LIFE HAPPENS

Live It!

Transforming Life's Challenges

into True Happiness

Jake French

ISBN: 978-615-39414-5
Printed in the USA   Cover Design by Deane's Graphics

To my mom,

without whom my life wouldn't be the same

Contents

Acknowledgments

Starting life over as a quadriplegic, author and inspirational speaker has been an unexpected and challenging change in my life. If it were not for the incredible support of family and friends, my life as I know it would not be possible. My mom, Margaret, has unselfishly changed her whole life to make mine better. She is the most wonderful person I know and I will never be able to thank her enough. At home, my dad Bill, keeps everything working and is crucial to our country lifestyle. My brother Brad is my best friend, the person who pushes me the most to live the best life I can.

My uncles and aunts support my family in so many ways. Uncle Dan encouraged me to set goals in life and Uncle Larry urged me to be an inspirational speaker, which coincidentally led to this book. I sincerely appreciate Aunt Rose Ann for her loving support and Aunt Kathleen for opening her home and heart.

All of the contributors to this book have gone through tremendous challenges in their lives and have come out on top. They are an inspiration to me and simply outstanding people!

Thank you to my mentors, Chuck and Candace Whitlock, for believing in me and helping me pursue my new direction in life.

My heartfelt appreciation goes to Jake Faris, who has been an essential part of my book writing team.

A big thank you to the Dufur community and the Dufur School District for the fundraisers and support our family received. Sheriff Craig Roberts, Sheri Magdlen and Mark Koberstein opened many doors, organized fundraisers and became enthusiastic advocates for me.

I truly appreciate the Holy Name Sisters for providing lodging and Adrianna Carr for assisting me with administrative services. In addition, Suzanne Bigelow, my wellness coordinator, has taught me how to relax with yoga.

I feel very lucky to have had such great care at Harborview Medical Center from nurses Melissa Psachos and Marta, as well as a great physical therapist, Jessica Wassman. All three played a big role in the positive attitude towards life that I have today. Justin, a night nurse at Oregon Health & Science University, changed my outlook on life at a crucial time with his kindness.

Once I got home it was time for more physical therapy at Mid-Columbia Medical Center in The Dalles. Anna Saltonstall was the best physical therapist I ever had. Not only did she do more to help me achieve my goals, she also became a personal advocate and good friend. She introduced me to her friend Jenny McCarty, who walked 1,000 miles on the Pacific Crest Trail for me, raising thousands of dollars for my physical therapy. Jenny, you rock!

With the help of many generous donations from family, friends and people I have never even met, I am able to improve my quality of life and continue my dream of walking again.

Since the first day after my injury, I have been surrounded by special friends who have traveled many miles to visit me and have taken the effort to stay in contact. To each and every one of you, thank you for getting me back to a place where I can enjoy life again. With an awesome support system such as mine, it is easy to find joy in each day!

From the bottom of my heart, to each of you, thank you.

Foreword

When I first met twenty-four-year-old Jake French, I wondered what, if anything, he could teach me that I didn't already know at my well-ripened age of 66.

Don't misunderstand me. I have a natural curiosity about life and the world I live in. I learn new things every day. For example, I just found out that an airplane's black box is orange, and that catgut actually comes from sheep or goat intestines.

After hearing Jake speak, I realized just how special he is if he can inspire an old guy like me.

We've all heard stories about young men and women accomplishing amazing things before turning 30. Did you know that our third President, Thomas Jefferson, was a successful lawyer at 24? With only 18 months of formal education, Abraham Lincoln became an Illinois state senator at 25. Most of us have heard about how entrepreneur and philanthropist Bill Gates dropped out of Harvard to start the company that would dominate the computer world. Tennis powerhouse Serena Williams claimed the singles title at the US Open at 18 and has never looked back. Anthony Robbins said he knew how to change the world and was teaching people how to change their lives long before he reached 30; he went on to coach U.S. Presidents and CEOs of major corporations.

What does all of this have to do with Jake French?

After you read Jake's story, you will understand. Like so many great men before him, he is wise for his years. He has an understanding about people and what motivates them. Like other successful young people, Jake French will inspire those who meet him. I predict that his name and story will become synonymous with his message of "Life Happens—Live It!" Those who have had the privilege of meeting him and hearing him speak won't easily forget his words.

The most profound quotes are often the simplest. I've always loved one that has been attributed to both Ralph Waldo Emerson and Oliver Wendell Holmes: "What lies behind us and what lies before us are tiny matters compared to what lies within us." (I guess if your quote is repeated by other famous people, attribution for the original quote can get a little murky.)

Jake French is the living embodiment of American author Charles R. Swindoll's statement, "Life is 10% what happens to you and 90% how you react to it." Swindoll summed up the importance of one's attitude when he wrote, "We are all faced with a series of great opportunities brilliantly disguised as impossible situations."

LIFE HAPPENS Live It! speaks volumes about Jake French and how he turned what most would see as an impossible situation into a great opportunity. It seems that no matter what the obstacle, Jake sees it as a challenge. Jake is living proof of Richard L. Evans' belief that nothing is unrealistic if you believe you can do it. And Jake shows his audiences how they, too, can do what they set their minds to.

No stranger to the devastating effects of physical limitations, Helen Keller said that only through trial and suffering could a person's soul be strengthened and success achieved. Jake views his physical limitations as simply a few more obstacles to climb over on his way to self-actualization and fulfillment.

Courage, determination and resolve can be created from within. When you read Jake's chapter, you'll know where his courage comes from. You'll understand why I hold Jake in such high esteem. And you'll also know how you can develop the same positive, can-do attitude.

Life takes us in many unforeseen directions. I'm reminded of the time my family and I cruised through the Panama Canal to visit a number of the islands in the Caribbean. Once through the Canal, we hurled a wax-sealed bottle full of photos, personal notes including our names and addresses, and some U.S. currency into the Caribbean Sea from our cruise ship. We had the romantic notion that the bottle would be taken by the currents and wash up on a distant shore decades later, where a stranger would find it and wonder, "Who were these people? Why did they throw this overboard?"

About six weeks later, we were surprised to receive a note from a U.S. citizen vacationing on the Mexican Riviera. She had found our bottle on the beach, minus the money we had put inside. Go figure. Evidently, the bottle had quickly traveled back through the Panama Canal where we had come from.

Life reminds me of that bottle. We put things into it that we think are important, including our expectations of what the future will hold. Then we're pitched onto a sea of uncertainty, never knowing exactly where we will end up or how we got there.

Jake earned his degree from the University of Idaho and planned to work outdoors as a forester in a career that would not have placed him in the public eye. The job in itself would probably not have caused a great deal of introspection or philosophical analysis. A freak accident and diagnosis that he was a quadriplegic sent Jake French in another direction. If Mohandas Gandhi, the Mahatma, had not been thrown off a train because he was an Indian and, therefore, considered a second-class citizen, would he have become the man who, by passive resistance, forever changed his nation's history?

Remember the 1992 movie *Lorenzo's Oil*? Based on the true story of Augusto and Michaela Odone, whose son had inherited a rare, fatal disease, the drama shows how the couple bucked the medical community's traditional approach to the disease. Frustrated by the failings of the experts, Lorenzo's parents decided to learn all they could about the brain disorder and Augusto figured out how to treat the disease more effectively than once thought possible. This great stride was accomplished by the sheer determination of two passionate parents with no prior experience in the field. Because of the outcome, could one conclude that it was a good thing that Lorenzo had the disease? Of course not. But Augusto's willingness to fight what was a death sentence for his son despite the unknown outcome and unanticipated costs—his job, his savings and almost his marriage—revealed a courage that cannot be denied.

In *LIFE HAPPENS Live It!* Jake will introduce you to other everyday heroes like W Mitchell. An adventurer, pilot, entrepreneur, sometime-politician and professional speaker, W Mitchell has faced one setback after another. His inspirational story is nothing short of amazing.

You'll meet Arielle Rausin, a remarkable young woman with a story of perseverance and determination to excel that you'll not soon forget. She believes that we each need to ask ourselves how we can use what we have instead of crying for what we've lost.

Ron Heagy brings audience members to their feet after his speeches. His 10-point "Never Give Up Creed" stresses the importance of tapping one's full potential and staying strong to the finish. How can someone facing such adversity master his attitude and choose to be positive each day?

Welcome to a world of ordinary people who have successfully transformed their lives after traumatic life-threatening incidents.

How do we acquire the same level of commitment in the absence of such a negative driving force? Without a serious illness, devastating accident or a life-changing loss, how can someone find and keep the attitude that makes a life truly successful? After my heart attack and bypass surgery years ago, I lost weight, lowered my cholesterol, began to eat sensibly and decided to shed the negativity—including the negative people and promote the positive in my daily life. Wouldn't it have been smarter simply to do these things before I experienced a life-threatening event? Certainly. Unfortunately, sometimes it takes a huge alarm, like a heart attack, to make us wake up to life.

Jake wants to wake you up before your alarm goes off. *LIFE HAPPENS Live It!* will give you the keys to living your best life, no matter what happens.

Chuck Whitlock

Author, Investigative Reporter and Speaker

An old Cherokee parable recounts the story of a grandfather speaking to his grandson about a battle that is waged inside of all people. The old man said that the battle is between two wolves.

He told the boy, "One wolf is evil. It is anger, envy, jealousy, regret, greed, arrogance, self-pity, guilt, resentment, inferiority, lies, false pride, superiority and ego." The boy's eyes grew wide as he listened.

"The other wolf is good. It is joy, peace, love, hope, serenity, humility, kindness, benevolence, empathy, generosity, trust, compassion and faith."

The young child pondered what his grandfather had said and asked, "Which wolf wins the battle?"

The old Cherokee replied, "The one you feed."

Anonymous

LIFE HAPPENS—Live It!

Last night I dreamed about how lucky I am to have become a forester, to be living my dream! The lush primordial forests with their powerful waterfalls, beautiful wildlife and cheerful wildflowers are right outside my window, welcoming me to work each morning. Suddenly, the picturesque scene and tranquility I am enjoying are dashed by a loud *snap*!

I'll never forget the sound my neck made when it broke. I even hear it in my sleep.

And then I wake up and see the Chair.

The Chair

The Chair stands in the corner of my bedroom. It quietly sits, waiting through the night for the beginning of another day. In the shadows, the dark green frame looks black. Fashion experts will tell you that black is "slimming," that dark colors are "understated." But there is nothing understated about the Chair. It's big. It's heavy. It's about as subtle as a chainsaw.

From my position on my bed, where I'm lying as I watch an episode of one of my favorite sitcoms, it's easy to see that chainsaws actually are a decorative theme in my room. John Deere toy chainsaws adorn the walls as do photos of me wielding chainsaws as I slice through large logs. A hand-drawn chainsaw on a note I made in third grade proclaims, "I want to be a logger when I grow up" in large, primary-school writing.

Other than the looming presence in the corner, wheelchairs are not a decorative motif here. No crayon sketches of big, dark wheelchairs, no notes describing a wish to be wheelchair bound are mingled among the chainsaw images. The neck injury, the paralysis, a life lived in a wheelchair—these were not part of my plan.

I laugh at another sarcastic comment from one of the TV show's characters, letting the stress of my day roll off in easy humor. It's a tradition for my mom, Margaret, and me to end our days with one or two episodes of our favorite sitcom. Like the show's main character, I enjoy providing humorous commentary during the frequent frustrations in life. My frustrations aren't the same as the fictional character's and I don't have a studio audience to appreciate my humor, but I can usually get my friends and family to crack a few smiles. Sprawled on my bed, laughing at the TV, you might not realize that this is a small respite from my duel with the Chair.

I know that tomorrow is another day that will bring numerous frustrations and a few small victories. But those small victories taste sweet. I make the decision every day that *I rule the Chair;* the Chair does not rule me.

My life is still my own.

Go Outside and Play!

I grew up with my family on five acres outside Eagle Creek, Oregon. Not much more than a crossroads for a feed store and an elementary school, Eagle Creek was perfect for us. My mom taught music at the elementary school and Bill, my dad, worked as a quality assurance inspector at Boeing of Portland, an aircraft manufacturer in Troutdale. With my younger brother Brad in tow, I would explore our large backyard, where trimmings and logs left by our dad turned into forts, and forts turned into adventure.

Ian (not his real name), a boy just a year older than me, lived across the road from us. He had a younger sister, Nancy (not her real name), who was almost as tough as we were and was Brad's age. I remember the four of us setting off on many explorations of the uncharted backyard. Before we left on an adventure, Brad and I would make sure we had all the equipment we might need. Preparing for our adventure was most of the fun! Later in life, as I prepared for a workday spent in a much larger forest, I sometimes thought about my gift for organization and pragmatism, natural traits that have served me well.

As a child, we had a Tupperware container, complete with a hand-drawn red cross, that contained solutions for every possible danger that lurked in the woods. I smile when I remember what we were worried about back then. Under the airtight Tupperware seal, we kept real "essentials." We even had a snake bite kit, even though there aren't any poisonous snakes in Eagle Creek. But, if I had anything to do with our plans, we were prepared for any possibility. At least that's what I thought.

There weren't any real estate developments, fences or roads that bordered our property. The forest beyond our five acres looked the same as the forest near the house. During one of our weekend adventures in the backyard, the four intrepid adventurers realized we had a slight problem.

We were lost.

My mom and dad were sitting on the back deck enjoying the afternoon when they heard our high-pitched voices growing more and more alarmed.

"Are we lost?" my parents heard from the woods.

"I'm scared," Nancy cried.

"Of course I know the way," I assured my young companions.

"Kids?" We stopped talking. Had it been an audible mirage? Was the forest now playing tricks on us?

"Kids, we're right here. Follow the sound of our voices and you'll come right to the house."

Mom!

We all started running toward my mom's voice at the same time. Mom gave us cool lemonade and eventually our nerves calmed down. Our ambitious exploration of the woods halted for a while, but in a matter of days the four of us were off on another mission into the fir and hemlock. This time I made sure a compass was included in the preparations. More importantly, I made sure I knew how to use it.

Our property in Eagle Creek was where my interest and love for the outdoors developed. I followed my dad around, learning about the forest environment as he maintained our land. Examining the stumps of old-growth Douglas fir, I felt like an archaeologist. Hundred-year-old methods began to reveal themselves. The chop marks on the side of a nine-foot-wide stump might look like funny bite marks but I learned that, in order to get above the swell (where they would be slowed down by excessive sap), the loggers would make ax cuts to place their springboards. Loggers stood on springboards while using a two-man crosscut saw. When I found myself struggling to cut a two-by-four with my little handsaw, I would imagine what life was like for loggers a century ago. It was the first time I thought about turning my love for the forest into a career.

I watched friends grow out of their dreams as they matured, but I never grew out of my love for the woods, maybe because I never ran out of fun things to do there.

Ian soon grew tired of the hikes through the woods and preparing emergency kits with me. I remember his family always having a variety of off-road machines around, four-wheelers mostly. Ian's dad had a dirt bike that we would watch him ride as we dreamed about having our own some day. Sure enough, soon Ian had his own dirt bike, a Yamaha YZ80. Engines and bike tracks became our obsessions.

When I was nine I got my own Kawasaki. It was a screamer, but a fast bike isn't the easiest one to learn on. When I brought it home I had visions of Ian and me tearing around our five acres looking for some gnarly jumps. I finally caught up to my best friend after school one day and told him the great news. Ian didn't act that thrilled.

"Great." Not *great!* Just *great.* Like the word fell off a cliff. I tried explaining it like I would to my younger brother.

"Well, it *is* great because you can bring your bike over and we can ride around the woods in the backyard. It'll be awesome!"

"I can't." Ian found something else to look at on the horizon.

"Why not?"

"No bike."

"Oh. What broke?" There's always something to fix on a dirt bike. That's what makes them so much fun. Ian's dad was always working on their four-wheelers and bikes. If he was working on Ian's bike then maybe we could head over to his garage and help. It was always fun to watch and learn the subtleties of two-stroke engine maintenance, and Ian's dad was good with his hands. It's how he got most of his jobs, which usually involved working with his hands or operating machinery.

"Nothing. My dad sold it." A little anticlimactic, but I got over it.

Ian's family still had their four-wheelers, so we managed to do a fair amount of tearing around the dirt trails. When Brad was old enough for his own dirt bike, our little gang grew to three members. Adventures on our bikes were about speed, mud and "air," the distance off the ground we could get from a jump.

Brad and I filled our free time with trail time. In many ways, it wasn't the same as our hikes through the backyard. We were older now, playing with miniature grown-up toys, but we were still adventuresome boys exploring the woods. When I went to sleep after a day of riding, I could still smell gasoline on my hands and hear the sharp pinging sounds of the two-stroke engines.

Like I can still hear the *snap* that would forever change my life.

In the sixth grade, I convinced my dad to take Brad and me hunting. Dad came along on that first trip during upland game season to make sure we observed all the lessons we had learned about firearm safety and proper hunting etiquette. After we passed his test, Brad and I had permission to hunt by ourselves. Mom and dad would drop us off with our gear and we'd stalk a stretch of wilderness, meeting them further down the road.

It wasn't so much about getting the grouse; it was about seeing parts of the wilderness I wouldn't normally see. Hunting with Brad, I not only found another way to appreciate the wilderness, but I also found someone who loved the outdoors just as much as I did.

As always, preparation was one of the best parts of our adventures. Early in our hunting experiences together, Brad and I decided to conduct a scientific survey prior to grouse season to determine the best possible hunting location. We spent a month of weekends hiking, notebook and pencil in hand. We cataloged the location of plant varieties and animal signs. We set out during different times of the day to note the best time for animal activities. Did our preparations make for the best hunting season on record? Not that I can remember. What I recall is how much fun it was, exploring nature with Brad at my side, pretending that we were discovering the animals and plants for the first time.

As a seventh grader, I remember my parents talking about retirement. My dad would be 55 in a couple of years and Boeing was offering him early retirement. He decided to take it, which sounded great to me. I liked the idea of my dad being around more. Then came the opening of fishing season.

The first day it was legal to catch trout in Oregon was a family holiday in the French household. Each year, on the first Saturday of April, my dad, Brad and I could be found on the shores of the Smock Prairie Reservoir near Wamic, Oregon. The night before opening day was full of excitement as we prepared our reels and tackle. In the morning, just like Christmas morning, Brad and I awoke early and started nudging mom and dad. We drove from Eagle Creek to the reservoir, stopping at the same bend of the White River where we always stopped to eat the egg-and-bacon croissants our mom had packed for breakfast. We fished until we either caught our limit or realized that no combination of casting and lures would entice the trout that day.

That year, my mom lost track of my dad along the side of the lake. Knowing how much he loves fishing, she started getting worried. When he reappeared from the access trail, she peppered him with questions. My dad explained that he'd been talking to some locals about a music teacher position in nearby Dufur. Unbeknownst to Brad and me, our parents had been considering a move to the east side of Oregon. They still wanted to be close to the urban conveniences in Portland but looked forward to a more rustic lifestyle. However, finding a job for my mom, who was still years away from eligible retirement age, was a key piece to the puzzle.

"Go talk to them!" my dad insisted.

She talked to the anglers. It sounded like she would have a shot at the job.

Trout in the ice chest and buzzing with the possibilities, we headed back toward Eagle Creek. In the car I remember my parents talking about the offer.

When we stopped at the Tygh Valley General Store for soft drinks and a snack, mom asked the cashier if she knew of anyone in the area who might be selling their house.

"Actually," she paused, "there was something I saw in the paper about a lot for sale up in Friend." Oregonians and our crazy names for towns. Boring, Weed, Damascus, Idea, Drain and Zig Zag are just a few.

After the cashier retrieved her last copy from the trash, we read, "Single-family ranch on forty acres of picturesque forest. Sixteen acres have been converted to Christmas tree farm. One outbuilding and barn or shop. Motivated seller." Each of us imagined what it must look like, this converted Christmas tree farm. The drive back was spent discussing the various merits of moving now or staying in Eagle Creek. Dad still had a year of work left and would face a time-consuming commute; the drive down the Columbia River was gorgeous but could become treacherous with ice and snow in the winter. Yet even he finally started getting excited. A consultation with the map showed that Friend was a tiny dot outside Dufur. It sounded perfect to me.

In a short time, my mom and dad sold the house in Eagle Creek and bought the property in Friend, which turned out to be a group of widely-dispersed properties near a town that had burned down decades earlier. Mom still didn't have a job after months of waiting and the occasional phone call from "the best-qualified music teacher in Oregon," she finally was hired as the new K-12 music instructor.

What Can I Dufur Ya?

Though I enjoy spending days at a time out in nature, I like people and always seem to find friends wherever I go. Ian and I stayed in touch for the first year I was living in Dufur. But as I became more engrossed in high school activities and summer jobs, we eventually drifted apart.

In Dufur, I discovered several boys my age with ATVs and dirt bikes. Even cooler, I made a few friends that were allowed to go out plinking with their rifles in the foothills. Talking with these friends and their dads, I picked up a few pointers about shooting and hunting. When Terry Boyer, an old friend from Eagle Creek, was staying at our house for a weekend, I was ready to show him a thing or two.

Terry and I were raw thirteen-year-olds the summer after my family moved to Dufur. Like many young men, we wanted to test our innate hunting prowess. Because of the danger that they pose to livestock and domestic pets, coyotes were the only animals in the state that needed to worry about hunters year-round. The two of us, armed with dedication, a scoped .22

rifle and a coyote call, were out to help the local ranchers and farmers.

Set against the unnatural backdrop of blacktop and cement, coyotes are easy to spot in an urban setting. Out in their natural environment, they're not so apparent. With their coloring and shifty movements, coyotes often seem to appear out of nowhere, but they're in a posture that lets you know they've been looking at you while you've been looking for them.

What we may have lacked in hunting experience we made up for in optimism. I hunkered down in nearby timber-company land near my house. Outside of the tree line—mainly Douglas fir and Ponderosa pines—was a field of tall grass. I set up with my rifle and Terry crouched next to me in the grass with the binoculars and the coyote call, which actually makes the sound of a wounded rabbit to attract the coyote. After taking a survey of the local dads, I had discovered that this was the recommended way to hunt coyotes. So we sat in the middle of the clearing, blowing a pitiful sound on our coyote call and checking the tree line for signs of our prey.

Diligently, we scanned the hillside, checking between the trees with binoculars. We took turns blowing on the distressed-rabbit call, eliciting different varieties of mournful mewing sounds: loud, short, long, soft. The minutes ticked by: 15, 30, 45, and still no coyotes appeared. Perhaps the local pack had other plans. Maybe easy rabbit meat wasn't on the menu. The sun was at the horizon and dusk was waiting to fall.

Ready to call it a night, we started to get up when Terry

and I saw the mountain lion at the same time. Nothing 50 yards away had ever looked so close before. Not wanting to cause an unnatural movement, our limbs froze. We slowly sank back down into the grass. The mountain lion didn't give a sign that it saw our movement; it was concentrating on a deer that had wandered into the meadow. We were in trouble now.

First, a small disclaimer about mountain lions. These large cats aren't "man-eating" predators. We knew that. Though they occasionally get into trouble for attacking humans, it's typically in areas where high-density developments cut into the cats' hunting territory. Someone out for a daily run along a park trail, listening to an iPod, can look like prey to a hungry mountain lion. I knew that if Terry and I tried to run away from this impressive predator, our small frames would look like dinner. I recalled an old joke about how you don't have to be faster than the bear, you only have to be faster than whoever else is running from the bear. I'm ashamed to admit it now, but I looked at Terry and wondered if I could outrun him. It's not like I was thinking about shooting him in the leg to get an advantage.

Realizing I needed a distraction, I whispered, "Do you think we should shoot it?"

"With a twenty-two? That would just make it mad." Terry had a point.

We watched the mountain lion as the day dimmed. The scope on my rifle brought the cat even closer. It was a scary predicament, yet at the same time we found it hard not to be amazed by the cat's terrifying beauty. Though the mountain lion probably outweighed me by 20 pounds, its graceful movements didn't make a sound and left the grass seemingly untouched.

As dusk settled and the cat crept closer to the deer, I realized that we were about to witness a mountain lion dining *al fresco*. Would it consider us a threat to its prey? I didn't want to wait around to find out.

"Wanna see if we can scare it?" I whispered to Terry.

"Not really." Terry replied, but gave a nod. It was our only real option.

I held up three fingers.

Then two.

Then one.

Watching the mountain lion for any signs of aggression, I jumped up with my rifle over my head and did my best imitation of a Tusken Raider from *Star Wars*.

"Blabloublablahbloobah!" I screamed as loud as I could.

Terry jumped up simultaneously and did his own crazy monkey dance.

The doe jumped three feet in the air and vanished. The mountain lion didn't budge. And then it sat down, now paying full attention to us instead of the deer.

Oh crud. I didn't know what else to do.

Terry got my attention and made shooting gestures.

I shook my head emphatically and then did my best impression of a cat bathing itself after dining on two tasty boys.

Terry shook his head. "No, right in front of it," he whispered.

I took a second to think about it before bringing up the rifle to my shoulder. Aiming at the ground just in front of the sitting animal, I emptied the ten-round magazine as fast as I could cycle the bolt.

Without the recoil from a larger rifle, I could watch the dust flying up in front of the mountain lion, who sat unfazed by the fireworks. Not knowing what to do next, as soon as we heard the click of a firing pin on an empty chamber, we did what any self-respecting person in our predicament would do: We ran.

No mountain lion attacks in Wasco County were reported that day, but two junior-high boys broke the record for the cross-country 800-meter dash, unofficially, of course.

The best way to put it, though it might sound crude, is that I'm a better hunter than I am a killer. Let me explain. Going out with the purpose of finding an animal in which to put a bullet, arrow or hook isn't the point. The point is to enjoy and appreciate the wilderness. Although this means different things to different people, for me it means both participating in nature's wonders and enjoying its bounty. It also comes with the responsibility of not wasting that bounty.

Growing up outside of Dufur, I picked up the natural rhythm of life. We learned from friends and neighbors about hunting and fishing. They gave us tips about planting and harvesting our garden. I also learned the best way to harvest the wood from our property for heat in the winter. Unlike so many urbanites, my direct connection with the resources I consumed instilled in me a respect for nature, which in turn reinforced my love for the world around me.

Terry has been by my side through hilarious adventures and gut-wrenching tragedy. It's the same with many of my friends. Seth Fargher was another kid my own age whom I met when I arrived in Dufur. Seth's passion, like the passion of all his family members, was getting on a four-wheeler and finding some backcountry trail to ride. His family was always packing up the trailer and heading off to China Hat, Rock Creek or Henderson Flats for the day or for a whole weekend. Often, my brother Brad and I were invited along.

One of our all-time favorite spots was China Hat, a volcanic cinder cone near Bend, Oregon. During one of our frequent trips, Seth and I were riding near the cone when I pulled ahead of him to get out of his dust trail. Seth caught up to me and found me off my bike, doing a poor imitation of the funky chicken.

"A bee! A bee's in my pants!!!" With that, I pushed my handlebars toward Seth and started fumbling with my belt buckle.

Being the good friend that he is, Seth gently set my bike on its side and then began frantically digging around in his backpack for his camera. I juggled my focus between ripping my pants off and trying to wrestle the camera from Seth's hands. Eventually the pants came off and after imparting a few welts, the unwanted insect flew off.

Unfortunately, Seth never let go of his camera. He occasionally reminds me that he still has the photo. I'm standing there, looking exhausted but relieved, with my pants around my ankles.

With the friends I made in my last year of junior high, going into high school felt like I'd lived in Dufur my whole life. For most grade school students, making the transition to high school is a big deal. It's a new school, with many more students crowding the hall. The school in Dufur was a little different. There weren't enough kids for separate schools. Kids from kindergarten through the 8th grade went to school in one hall of the building; high school students used another hall. Sometimes, like for gym class or music, you even had the same teacher. Mrs. French, as my mom was known in the school, was the music teacher; she was also the choir director, band conductor, art and home economics teacher, and sole director of the spring all-school Broadway musical production. It was rare not to find Mom working on some project in the kitchen until the wee hours of the morning. With a classroom in the high school, she was always nearby—just what every teenage boy dreams of.

My graduating class made up twenty-four of the nearly 250 kids at the school, so the typical homogenous cliques that make such good television and movie fodder weren't a part of our lives. No six degrees of separation existed in Dufur; it was more like two. Parents could keep close tabs on us, but their ability to find out where their kids were and what they were doing actually afforded us a certain amount of freedom.

Maybe it was the watchful eye of our parents, or the fact that the twenty-four students in my class kept busier than most, but we kept our noses clean throughout high school. The typical trouble that teenagers find—drinking and drugs—wasn't a big factor with my friends. One or two kids in our high school might have used some recreational drugs, but we all knew who they were and what they were up to. Although drinking eventually would become an important weekend pastime of mine in college, I stayed away from the kids in high school who used or abused drugs of any sort.

As a kid looking for spending money and ways to help out friends and neighbors, I had a steady gig as local grunt and handyman. Heading into the summer between my junior and senior years, I realized that occasional work as a handyman wasn't going to cover my growing expenses. I started thinking about making some real money.

John Odegard, the owner of Deschutes River Adventures, a local river-rafting company, decided to take a chance on me and hired me as a rental-raft gopher. My actual job title was "rubber monkey."

While I could have come up with a more important sounding title, like "rental equipment service and supply specialist," I eventually realized that rubber monkey was both a title and an honorific. I learned the job quickly, but getting the rafts to and from the rental customers was hard work in the summer heat. The first thing I learned was that John didn't micromanage, nor did he accept excuses. He expected me to do my job right the first time. It's a lesson that stuck.

I got to the job in the cold morning hours of summer and

began patiently prepping for the day. Failing to get an order right meant that I would have to make the round trip back to the warehouse for the missing equipment; if a customer had been inconvenienced, it could mean that John would be making the personal trip out to the river to apologize. I knew that wouldn't bode well for me.

I didn't mind making a few mistakes if it meant I would do the job better in the future, and I think John appreciated my responsible approach to work. Down the road I learned that a recommendation from John could open doors.

I graduated from high school in 2004 with a 3.8 GPA. To help with the cost of college, I applied for and was awarded several scholarships. The one that made me proudest was the Jerri Walker DePriest scholarship. The Jerri Walker DePriest Memorial Endowment Fund was the final legacy of a woman whose joyful life and positive outlook—despite enduring 18 years of treatment for cancer—touched all who knew her.

The 100-Year-Old Club

After high school I continued to build toward my dream of turning my love for nature into a career.

Although many people who live outside of Oregon would claim that the state is best known for being the home of Nike and Intel, I would say that it should be best known for its vast forests. Folks who love the outdoors think they have discovered paradise when they first see the beauty of Oregon. From the heights of Multnomah Falls and the depths of Crater

Lake to its eastern deserts and rugged ocean cliffs, it's an amazing place to explore. From hunting and fishing to skiing and river rafting, the state has it all. I felt extremely fortunate to be born in such a wonderful place. As I began college, I felt my career aspirations starting to become reality and my dream was within reach.

I was accepted into the University of Idaho's Forest Products program, and my freshman year in Moscow, Idaho, was full of firsts, including the first time I had lived away from my family. The other students in the Forest Products program were a tight-knit group of seriously self-sufficient types. They made me feel right at home.

As a Forest Products newbie, I was asked if I'd like to join the Logger Sports Team. In existence for nearly 100 years before my arrival, the club's official name was the Associated Foresters of the University of Idaho. At regular meets, the UI team faced teams from other colleges in competitions ranging from throwing a double-bladed ax at a target (ax throwing) and tossing large logs (caber tossing) to climbing up a slanted pole with a chainsaw and cutting through a log at the end (obstacle pole). A multitude of different kinds of chopping contests included using a traditional cross-cut saw with either a teammate or solo to cut through a log (double and single buck).

Ax throwing? Caber tossing? I signed right up.

In Dufur, I had enjoyed the outdoor activities my environment provided, but the Department of Forest Products at UI was the big leagues. It's where I learned the science, acquired the skills and got the practice necessary to fulfill my dream. It was more fun than I could have imagined!

My first year, the Logger Sports Team boasted only 11 members and we had to wear a few different hats. I volunteered for the job of Equipment Steward, but two ratty chainsaws, some rusty cross-cut saws and axes were all I had to take care of. I'm not saying it was all my doing but, by the end of my four years at UI, the membership of the Logger Sports Team more than doubled. We added four new chainsaws to the equipment locker along with several more shiny axes and traditional saws.

During my junior year, the team hosted the Association of Western Forestry Clubs (AWFC) Forestry Conclave, the World Series of logging sports on the west coast. As organizers, we supplied the lodging, the facilities, even the logs. The Western White pine is the official tree of Idaho but, because of the deadly blister rust epidemic, it's also one of the rarest types of lumber. The Forest Sports team located some and they were a hit. It turns out that just about any type of saw, cheap or expensive, old or new, *flies* through the wood of the White pine tree.

I did well in my best events, ax throwing and double buck. We placed third, but the final results didn't reflect how well we moved that buck saw through our log. Worse than getting third place was getting beaten by my younger brother Brad and his teammate. If my partner and I hadn't stopped for a few seconds to look at our stuck saw—which still bugs me—we probably would have taken home the gold medal.

I spent the summer between my freshman and

sophomore years back in Dufur working for John Odegard as a rubber monkey and saving up for an apartment. In my sophomore year, some friends from the team and I moved into a cruddy dive on A Street which we affectionately called "the A-hole." As poor college students we lived well on what Mother Nature provided. I remember the barbeque always stoked and an abundance of local steelhead, salmon and venison in preparation. Between my friends and a freezer we ate pretty well all year long. We also drank a lot of beer and, truth be told, almost anything else we could put our hands on.

One of the misconceptions that many Forest Products students ran into is that foresters are loggers. We probably fueled the confusion by running around with axes and crosscut saws for fun. Just as people who grow grapes aren't necessarily the same people who make the wine, loggers and foresters are different. Being a forester is not just about Carhartts and chain saws. Foresters know how to harvest trees, but we learned a little more than how a two-stroke chain saw works. Biology lies at the root of our discipline. The program throws in some engineering and chemistry so that we learn how consumers—builders, paper makers and even weekend do-it-yourselfers—use forest products. To get the products from the forest down the mountain, we also picked up some physics and logistics.

The program at the University of Idaho was built around getting its students started in a career. That meant internships. Between my sophomore and junior years, I was hired by the Washington State Department of Natural Resources as a seasonal silvicultural technician (also known as a paid intern). It was the first time someone paid me to do what I loved. It's not that every day was easy, but as each day started I took my time, prepared for each task and thought about the lessons I'd learned from John Odegard. John hadn't forgotten me either, according to my supervisor.

"That reference you gave me from the rafting company? John couldn't say enough about you. It's why you're here." I felt John's long arm of respect reaching out to me.

When summer came around again I went back to my Washington state internship. Following graduation, I applied for a job with the Idaho Department of Lands, where I worked out of the forestry office in St. Maries, near Coeur d'Alene. While I wasn't a full time employee there, they didn't exactly treat me like an intern. I got a state rig—an old Chevy pickup—complete with bald tires, trash-filled bed and an engine that would barely start!

My college years were made up of great times. My life was exciting as I worked to complete my final year of school. It also included some pretty close calls. One night, after drinking until 1:00 a.m. with several friends, we found ourselves on an icy road. Despite having a designated driver, our car spun out of control in the middle of an icy curve. The car rolled and we eventually slid into a ditch, having missed a telephone pole by inches. None of us was hurt, despite the fact that nobody was wearing a seatbelt. My theory at the time was that the alcohol had kept us limber and sitting tightly together probably kept us pinned in. With hindsight, I can see that my close calls were the result of too much partying. Merely being out in the wee hours puts a person at a great risk for "just being there" incidents; add alcohol and the mix can be dangerously potent.

Seven months later, another alcohol-fueled accident occurred around one in the morning. Driving at about 60 mph, our vision impaired and reflexes slowed by an excessive amount of alcohol, we hit a soft shoulder on a river road, ending up in the middle of a farmer's field. Miraculously, we had missed careening into the numerous trees or driving into the river.

It wasn't unusual for me to drink 10 to 15 beers a night. I was young, strong and, like everyone else I knew, I believed I was invincible. Everything we did was to the extreme, but nobody ever got really hurt, so what was the harm?

A short time later, a drunk driver would hit Rodney, one of my good friends, while he and I were changing a woman's tire. Working on the side of the road, we had no time to respond and nowhere to hide. Despite being thrown onto the hood of the disabled car, Rodney was lucky, only suffering a hairline fracture in his hip. Somehow I survived without a scratch.

Alcohol would play a huge role in the direction my life took five months later. I would find out how fragile one's body can be, and I would be invincible no longer. In a split second, my whole life would be turned upside down, and my luck would run out.

Working as a seasonal employee after my graduation was a smart move. I had on-the-job experience from my internships. I had graduated with honors. I was currently working in Idaho as a seasonal forester. Job hunting looked promising. While I'd worked in Washington and Idaho, my heart was still set on getting back to Oregon. That summer I finally got a the call from the Oregon Department of Forestry to work as a Natural Resource Conservation Specialist 1 (a fancy name for a forester) at the Tillamook Forest station near the Oregon coast.

It couldn't have been a more perfect situation. I wasn't a stranger to Tillamook. My grandmother Mary was born in Tillamook, and I had attended many family reunions at the Swiss Hall there. My Aunt Bernice, my grandmother's sister, still lived in Tillamook and I looked forward to visiting her. I'd spent summers exploring the beach at Rockaway and fishing the coastal lakes. In a way it was like coming back home. Mike Dwyer, a friend from college, had graduated a semester earlier than me and was already working in Tillamook. As poor college grads working in the same job at the same station, we decided to pool our resources. On November 10th I moved from the chilly mountains of Idaho to the damp cow-country of Tillamook, Oregon. Mike and I found an apartment and I tried getting re-acclimated to the rain. The station where we worked averaged 120 inches of rainfall a year. Rain gear became our regular uniform.

Looking back on that month in Tillamook, I should never have complained about the incessant rain. Today, I would welcome feeling cold, wet socks on my feet. I would relish having tired muscles after a hard day's work. But at the time I had no way of knowing that my life was about to change forever.

The Old Friend

Less than a month had gone by since I started working for the State of Oregon. Mike's birthday was coming up and, since he was far away from friends and family, I asked him if he wanted to spend his birthday in my old hometown of Eagle Creek. This conflicted with my Aunt Bernice's dinner invitation the same night, but I decided that having dinner with some of my old grade-school friends and listening to a local band would be a more proper celebration. When I told Aunt Bernice of my plans for the evening, she warned me, "Be careful, and don't get into any trouble with the police."

On Friday, December 5th, we drove to Eagle Creek after work for dinner and dancing. Even Terry, my old hunting buddy from Eagle Creek, joined us. New friends met old friends and, by the end of the evening, everyone was having a good time. We drank and I danced with Terry's older sister Rhonda, whom I had known since first grade. We really tore up the dance floor. Juiced by some great country music and alcohol, I swung her around until I was exhausted. I had no idea that the last dance of the evening would be my last dance *period*.

Mike, Terry and I piled into Terry's friend's truck and headed to the local mini-mart for gas and a pit stop. As the tank filled, the driver went in to pay and Terry went with him. Mike was doing his best impression of an exhausted birthday boy and I took in the scenery as I remembered walking to this mini-mart to buy candy as a kid. Brad, Ian and I were the three amigos back then. I was sorry that I had lost touch with Ian throughout high school and college. In my mind's eye, I could almost see a grown-up version of him stumbling away from the gas station lights into the darkness.

Hold on. That really *was* Ian. I got out of the pickup. "Ian!"

My childhood best friend spun around, off balance.

"Jake?" Ian swayed as he walked over to me. "You're sure bigger than you used to be." Ian reached out and patted my stomach. It was an odd thing to say and an even odder gesture to make. I started wondering where my friends were.

Looking around, with my back turned, I suddenly felt hands snake between my arms and sides. Before I could break free, Ian's hands were clasped behind my neck. He had me in a full nelson, with my shoulders pinned back and my head thrust forward.

It was obvious to me now that Ian was really drunk. Of course, my friends and I had been out celebrating, too, and I was in no shape to be wrestling. I was about to say something when suddenly Ian pitched us both forward. In his death grip, I couldn't move my arms to catch myself, and my inebriated boyhood friend couldn't react fast enough to release his grasp of me.

My head hit the ground first. As Ian came down on top of me, I heard an abrupt *snap* that resonated in my head.

Hitting my head the way I did, I was expecting unconsciousness, but I didn't black out. All I could see were the fluorescent gas station lights.

"Oh, man. Oh, man. Oh, man," Ian kept chanting as he disentangled himself from my limbs. "Stop goofing around! You're fine."

I didn't know what he was talking about. I couldn't feel anything. I couldn't even lift my head to see what was going on.

"I'm really hurt. Something's wrong."

"You're faking it!" he said, as he tried pulling me up.

I didn't feel my arms snatched by his hands, but my view of the gas station roof bounced and lurched.

"C'mon, man, knock it off. It's not funny!" Ian's eyes were bouncing back and forth from my face to the mini-mart door to the gas pumps.

"Knock what off? I'm not doing anything. Stop it, Ian. Something's not right." The swaying stopped for a second and Ian's face came into view. I saw him look toward the door of the mini-mart, and then I heard Terry's voice.

"What happened?" A note of alarm crept into Terry's usually calm voice.

"Terry, man, it's crazy. I was just horsing around, ya know? I think he's faking it." The words came out in a rush and the sound of terror appeared in his voice.

"Put him back down," Terry commanded. Another lurch and I was looking up into Terry's worried face.

"How bad is it?" I asked. I kept hoping that I couldn't be hurt that bad since I was still conscious.

Terry looked me in the face. "You're going to be fine."

I could hear someone yelling about calling 911 and then

a voice telling Ian to get lost.

"I've got you, Jake. Hold on." Terry was trying to get me to focus.

Terry reached over and brought his hand into view. Tightly clenched in his fist was my own hand. Those were my fingers. That was the dirt I missed with the scrub brush. Those were my calluses. But I couldn't feel Terry's hand.

"I can't feel anything." That's when I started to worry.

My Biggest Adventure

Arriving at about the same time as a car from the Clackamas County Sheriff's Department, the ambulance carried me to nearby Eagle Creek elementary school where I remembered many days playing on the swings. From the playground at the school, I was transported by helicopter to Oregon Health and Sciences University (OHSU) in Portland. The medical staff at OHSU took x-rays of my neck and found my spinal cord pinched between the sixth and seventh vertebrae. My neck was broken. With the force of my fall and the way Ian had attempted to get me upright, the two vertebrae looked like askew stepping stones.

My first surgery, where they installed a "halo" or brace stabilizing my head and neck, took place almost immediately. By the time I was out of surgery my parents had arrived from Dufur. When I regained consciousness, a surgeon explained to us what had happened to me physically and what the next steps were. I would undergo a second surgery to fuse the vertebrae in my neck together. Though I had no use of my limbs, I could still breathe and swallow.

He explained that it would be a tricky surgery. I might wake up on a breathing tube or without the ability to swallow. The surgery would start as soon as possible.

Finally left alone with my family, I unsuccessfully attempted turning to my mom, who was crying quietly next to my bed. I learned that trying to make even the smallest movements would take some getting used to.

"Look, guys. Chill. It is what it is. Let's get on with it. Everything will be okay," I said.

"How can you say that? How can you be so calm? Look what he did to you!" she yelled in anger.

"It happened. We'll get through this. Just stay strong. You'll see." Suddenly, I had found my strength and became the forceful one in the room. I didn't want my family and friends to be afraid. I didn't know where my courage was coming from, but I didn't feel any fear. The doctors were going to take care of the surgery. They would do whatever they could. *After* the surgery would come the hard part, the part that was completely up to me.

I woke up the morning of December 6th a different man. I had no feeling below my collar bone. I couldn't move my legs, feet, arms or hands. I could still breathe on my own and, judging by my stomach, soon I was going to test how well I could eat. Seth, my old friend from Dufur, had brought breakfast: one of everything from the McDonald's menu because he didn't know what I would be hungry for. As my mom forked syrupy pancakes into my mouth, I greeted my well-wishers.

Everyone was there. *Everyone*. From the University of
Idaho where he was following in my footsteps in Forest
Products, Brad arrived with all of my friends still living in
Moscow. Five coworkers from the Tillamook forestry station—
guys I had only known for three weeks—came by to see me. My
friend Whitney Hammel had raised the alarm in Dufur and all of
my high school friends visited me. For months she would keep
my Dufur friends informed of my progress via email. Along with
my family, my friends from the previous night had kept vigil
while I recovered from my surgeries.

Terry's sister Rhonda filled me in on what had happened
since the gas station event. Ian was in jail, but he had been
picked up that night on other charges having nothing to do with
our encounter. As a nurse, Rhonda understood why my body
went into convulsions after my neck snapped. Apparently, it's a
common symptom of an injury like mine, which may have
confused Ian into thinking I was playing a joke. No charges
against Ian for endangering another person or for reckless
behavior would be forthcoming because it could not be proven
that he had intended to hurt me.

To this day, I have not heard from nor seen Ian.

After the second surgery, a doctor came to my room and
discussed the prognosis with my family and me. I would be a C6
quadriplegic or "C6 quad" for the rest of my life. The doctor
explained that this could mean no use of my upper or lower
limbs ever again. He painted a bleak picture of catheters, hours

of physical therapy and a life totally dependent on others for even the most basic functions. My parents were in shock.

That night I lay awake. My mind felt like it was balanced above a pit of black, sticky depression. I tried to stay positive, to think about the possibilities of healing or finding a cure for my spinal cord damage. Suddenly the medical research headlines that had always been in the background of my life seemed much more important. My positive attitude and pragmatism teamed up to keep me balanced on the ledge. But the realization of what the future would be and the intensely negative prognosis of the doctor were trying to push me off balance, down into the pit.

It was half past three in the morning and I was unable to fall asleep, wondering if I should still try to drift off or just give up. A shadow fell across the doorway to the hall, and a guy in scrubs quietly walked in.

"Still awake?" he asked. I don't know how he knew. It's not like I could move much. My posture was the same, sleeping or awake.

"Yeah." My voice woke up my dad, who was sleeping in the chair next to my bed.

"Who are you?" I asked the stranger.

"Justin, your graveyard shift nurse." OHSU is both a university and a general hospital, which meant that most of my nurses at this point had been young, female, and cute. Needless to say, Justin was not what I was expecting and certainly not what I was hoping for.

"I've met Bill," Justin said as he gave my dad a nod, "but

49

this is the first time I've actually gotten to talk to you. How are you feeling?"

"Tired, but not sleepy."

"That's understandable. It's rough, these first few days." He walked over to the wall and turned some of the lights on, giving the room a half-lit glow. He started looking through the cabinets, collecting odds and ends.

"When was the last time you washed your hair?"

I had to think. "The night it happened. I took a shower after work before we drove to Eagle Creek."

"So it's been a few days?"

"I guess." That fact alone brought its own little dose of depression.

"That's what I figured." Justin rolled his eyes and smiled, grabbed a stool and wheeled over to my bed with his hands full of supplies. "The surgeons are masters at putting what's broken back together, though they sometimes overlook important details. Like clean hair."

Justin began maneuvering things around until a basin sat underneath my head. Using warm soapy water, he gave my head a thorough yet gentle scrub. Since the violence that had caused my neck to break, the only things that had been done to me were medically necessary. Was washing my hair necessary? Probably not. But the sensation of a warm, damp towel wiping the soap off one of the last areas of my body I could still feel was pure luxury.

But Justin wasn't done.

"Feel a little better?" Justin asked as he put things away.

"Much."

"Not quite tired yet?"

"No, but that's okay. Morning is around the corner."

"Well, until it gets here, let's see what's on TV. Pass me the remote, Bill. You guys like sports, right?"

After having my hair washed by another guy, of course I agreed that watching sports is just about the best thing to do. ESPN was one of the only sports channels not airing infomercials, so it was the international yo-yo championship for my dad, Justin and me. Justin sat there with us, marveling at the intense competition.

A simple act of kindness not only changed the course of my day but it also altered my outlook on the new life I faced. It's true that most of us will never realize what impact we have on others, but never discount the power of even the most modest acts of compassion.

Justin's contribution to my recovery might seem a tiny one. He washed my hair and we watched professional yo-yo players. But the experiences during that night will be with me for the rest of my life. I had spent hours lying there, feeling sorry for myself and sliding further and further into the quicksand that is depression. Justin's kind touch brought me out of my dark thoughts. Having my hair tenderly washed by another guy isn't something I'd have volunteered for prior to my injury. It's certainly nothing that I would have admitted to enjoying. But after days of medical procedures and stress, the gentle act was an entirely different experience.

My dream of being a full-time forester as I had imagined was over. I wouldn't be able to walk the old trails, fish the rivers and lakes, hunt or hike the wilderness like I used to do. Waking up under a canopy of old-growth trees while listening to the orchestration of bird songs swell around me was a thing of the past. Yet I no longer felt like wallowing in self-pity. I began to have new dreams and aspirations.

Thanks to Justin, that night I realized that, although my life was not going to be the same, it wasn't over. Thanks to physical therapy, I can wash my hair on my own now, but the lesson goes beyond simple hygiene. For all I knew, Justin was the first of many hair-washers and caregivers. Even now, I have to accept the fact that there are thousands of things I'll probably never do again. That fact does not mean that my life is over, worthless or that there aren't experiences that won't bring me a sense of adventure, pleasure, or fulfillment. Back from the brink of depression, I still had a lesson or two to learn about happiness, but that night was when I started thinking about how perspective and experience go hand in hand.

My whole life, when hiking, riding dirt bikes, hunting or working in the forest, I've always focused on what works. Some people call it pragmatism. I call it common sense. Up to that point in my life, I wasn't very experienced with depression; there wasn't much of a reason for it. After my injury, I could see that staying away from pity and depression was going to be a constant battle. I wasn't going to use alcohol to have a good time or to prop me up. Although it might have contributed to my becoming a C6 quad, I was not going to let alcohol paralyze me from the neck *up*. I've always tried to find what works, and depression just doesn't work for me. Depression and pity aren't going to "cure" me. They're not going to help me recover. They're not going to help me enjoy the future.

I realized that the biggest adventure in my life, living as a quadriplegic, was going to take both mental and physical preparation.

Past Tense

After only four days in the intensive care unit at OHSU, I was well enough to be transferred to the inpatient physical rehabilitation program at Harborview Trauma Center in Seattle. It was time to start the real work.

The physical therapy wing, where my mom and I lived, was quad, para (paraplegic) and stroke central. This is where those of us who have suffered from traumatic nerve damage can restart our lives. I remember the feeling of community, the sense that the doctors, nurses and therapists were all working toward one goal. Even the smallest success was a reason to celebrate. I had my share of small victories after my surgery at OHSU. The swelling in my spinal cord came down and, with therapy, I'd gained some use of my arms and very limited use of a few muscles in my hands.

Along with those victories came the realization that almost everything I enjoyed in life up to that point was gone.

Quads don't fish, don't hunt, and don't work as foresters. As that realization sank in, my attitude started slipping. What was the point of living if you can't do what you love? What was the point if life had to be lived in a wheelchair?

Though I kept a cheery facade, those types of dismal thoughts started flashing through my brain. One day, in between workouts, I was sitting in my chair outside of the gym listening to a patient complain. She was my age or just a little older, dressed in matching warm-ups and talking to a trainer about the embarrassment of her disability. She looked like a cheerleader to me, and I wondered how someone so young and fit had suffered from a stroke. She was in therapy to overcome a slight paralysis of her left side that gave her the cutest hitch in her step. She was explaining to the trainer that her life was hopeless. All the things she wanted to do were impossible now. Her life was ruined.

Although the complaints sounded familiar, they sounded downright ridiculous coming from her glossy lips. I hadn't felt my legs in months, and walking around with a little hitch in my step sounded pretty good! Rolling down the hallway I started looking around and, for the first time, really seeing what was there: a C4 quad that would never breathe on his own; a burn victim in another room; an amputee getting used to his new prosthetic; a stroke victim without the ability to speak. Times were bad and things were hard all over. All around me were people who would work their whole lives to gain back the amount of mobility that I have today.

I started hearing about other people who had

experienced remarkable successes through physical rehabilitation. As a young man, Michael Schwass had broken his neck during a high-school hockey game. He later survived three near-death experiences. Now a professional speaker, Michael can stand on his own as he delivers his inspirational message more than thirty years after his injury.

I started thinking about what happens in life and what makes people happy. At one end of the spectrum, I saw patients at Harborview who couldn't move anything below the neck and required ventilators to breathe. Should they be happy or unhappy? What about the burn victim? Judging from the attitudes that I could see, what happened to people and how they responded to it weren't necessarily related. I've heard people talk about how they don't like hospitals because what they see there makes them sad. After all the time I've spent wheeling through the halls of Harborview, I can see what they mean. Yet, for every sad scene, there is a happy one. Glorious victories, as small as they may seem to those in good health, take place every day in the hospital.

Life happens—that's what I realized at Harborview. It happened to me. It happened to everyone staying there. But what should we do about it? I started wondering if my response to my injury was more significant in my future development than the actual injury.

I stopped thinking about what I couldn't do. I stopped dwelling on the humiliations of life as a quad. I started returning to my old self. Humor has always been one of my strongest coping mechanisms, and soon the wisecracks started slipping out. The laughter came back.

Having my family around me helped. My mom slept on a couch in my room while my dad stayed with family in Seattle. Brad was on Christmas break from the University of Idaho, which meant that we all would celebrate Christmas together with my relatives in Seattle. Brad found a cedar twig to stand in for a tree which we stood up in an empty pop can, and festive strands of lit bears, deer, and red and green shotgun shells from Cabela's decorated the walls. We soon found out what the locals thought of our country decorating when I caught another patient's visitor staring at our display of holiday spirit. Because of the gun shells hanging around the room, she thought I might be part of a gang. I explained to her that I was about as far from being a gang member as Mother Teresa.

"Where I'm from, the only drive-by shootings we have are during deer season," I joked. Okay, so I wasn't ready to headline my own Comedy Central special, but it was a start.

As my physical therapy progressed, my dad headed back to Dufur to start remodeling the house so my wheelchair and I could move in after therapy. While I was stretching, gripping and lifting in the gym at Harborview, my dad was getting his exercise working on the house. A ramp needed to be built. My dad also added an accessible bathroom to my old room. Terry, his dad and his brother-in-law, along with several friends from Dufur made sure my dad didn't have to make all the modifications alone. Close friends and family have always made my journey easier.

The small victories at Harborview added up, and I "graduated" from their program after an eleven-week stay. But, to be honest, leaving the floor was frightening. In the hospital, we were loosely yet closely supported and supervised by medical staff. They set our schedules and, when things didn't go right, they were a call away. Wheeling out the doors of the hospital meant I was wheeling into my future, but I didn't know what the future held. What work could I get? What would it be like living back at home? Would my new life be a happy one?

Life had happened to me. Now it was time for me to live it on my own terms.

Rolling Forward

At first, life in Dufur was scary. As soon as we pulled into the carport, I realized just how extensive dad's remodel had been. To this day, I don't know how he managed it all. The ramp, bathroom and larger bedroom helped with the accessibility issues, but we were miles and miles from the nearest medical facility. Eventually, we determined that we could do it on our own, just my mom, my dad, my brother and me. We figured out our schedule and started accumulating therapy equipment. We really didn't have any space for it, so it all went into the living room, which jokingly became known as "Jake's Gym."

I noticed that my black cat Lefty was taking an extraordinary interest in me and my new circumstances. Although she and our other ferocious feline Poncho had always been considered true members of our family, Lefty became an even greater part of my life. She would leap into my lap and nuzzle me gently. When lying on my bed, I'd thump on my chest and she would jump on me, finally settling down over my heart. Her rhythmic purring relaxed and soothed me, de-stressing me as she kept me company. Studies have shown that animals can positively influence people on many levels, including lowering a person's blood pressure and elevating one's mood. After I returned home, Lefty seemed to concentrate her attention on me rather than anyone else in my family. The love of an animal can be a powerful force, and Lefty has become more than a pet to me: she's become a true, trusted companion.

I divided my day between exercise and research. I wanted to learn as much as I could about my injury and what I could do to overcome it. During my therapy, I thought about injury-related questions I need to research and talked to my mom (who had quit her job at the school to become my caregiver); in the afternoon, I did my research online and over the phone. For me, "overcoming" my injury didn't mean finding a cure or waiting for a miracle; it meant accepting that life had happened to me—I had become a C6 quad—and finding a way to move on. My injury happened. Past tense. I realized that I wasn't interested in dwelling on my injury. What I was interested in was *living*!

I was still unsure about my future. With some help, I could live life outside of the hospital, but I still didn't know what I was going to do with my life. I felt like a movie someone had paused. Other than exercises and research on the Internet, there wasn't much to do at home. Most of the kids who grew up with me planned to leave Dufur when they graduated. When you're into the outdoors, Dufur is actually a perfect place to live; skiing, fishing, hiking, hunting and rafting are only a few of the outdoor activities readily available. For a quadriplegic in a heavy motorized chair, these activities aren't exactly on your to-do list.

When I wasn't doing my therapy exercises, I sat in the Chair and thought about the warm summer activities that I couldn't do. When I wasn't sitting around thinking about what I was missing, I was distracting myself with movies and YouTube videos. I thought about my friends who weren't around. Even if they were around, what could I have done with them? We might go out to eat in nearby Maupin, but that would require a ride from the hardest-working taxi driver and caregiver in Dufur. In fact, if I wanted to hang out with anyone, it basically meant my mom would come along, too.

I spent my first summer in the Chair trying not to think about all the things I *couldn't* do. When I thought about those things I *could* do, I didn't want to be an inconvenience to anyone. I was pretty frustrated.

In August, Nicole (not her real name), a friend from high school, called me. Her family lived down the road from our property, which basically made us neighbors. In fact, since we caught the bus at the same stop, she was one of the first friends I made in Dufur. In our last year in school, she started dating a junior, whom she eventually married. The last I'd heard they were separated and she was living with their son in another state. She was one of the last people I expected to hear from, but she was calling to say she was in town.

"When did you get back?" I asked.

"The custody part of my divorce needs to be finalized, so I have to be here in person. I heard about what happened."

"Oh, yeah." Hearing her voice had distracted me for just a moment.

"I am so, so sorry," Nicole said.

"Oh, it's not your fault. Life just happens." My voice sounded flat in my ears.

"Do you want to get together? I'd love to see you," Nicole said.

"Come over! I was just thinking that this is a perfect afternoon to share with an old friend."

And she did. We sat in "Jake's Gym" and talked about our lives and what had happened to us since high school. Nicole's ambitions had always exceeded what Dufur could offer. Her olive skin and large, expressive eyes had always lent her a glamorous, worldly look. Not that I had ever really thought of her romantically. She had always just been the girl next door. I don't know if it was the time apart or the time I'd been alone at the house, but that day I took a second look at Nicole. And then I forced those impossible thoughts out of my head.

Since leaving Dufur, Nicole had settled on the East coast. She didn't expect the divorce process to take too long. She gave it a month. In the meantime, we hung out. It's not that she had a lot of choices, given that most of our peers were gone, but it never seemed like I was an inconvenience or that she would rather be somewhere else. In fact, she didn't seem to care at all about my paralysis or wheelchair.

We always managed to come up with things to do. What helped was that she had her son, Tom (not his real name), with her almost all the time, and most of the things I had been pining for weren't things you could take a four-year-old to do anyway. Dates were usually simple yet fun: picnics in the park, swimming at my water therapy, watching a movie while Tom played on the floor with old toys my mom had unearthed. I had been working on what's called transferring, getting my posterior from my chair to another surface using what muscles I could still control. Hanging out with Nicole gave me some extra motivation. If I could transfer, I could sit next to her on the couch. Better yet, if I could transfer to the driver's seat of the van, I could do the driving.

I worked on my transferring during the day and I'd usually invite Nicole and Tom over to hang out in the evening. While Tom didn't really trust me around his mom, he thought that my chair was pretty cool. He called it my "bike" and always asked if I would have my bike or be taking my bike. For my sessions of pool therapy, Nicole and Tom would tag along. That's when I saw her in a bikini for the first time. I swear, I almost felt my legs.

The issue of dating finally came up one day with my mom while I was trying to transfer from my wheelchair to the front seat of the van. It was only my 5,857th try.

"Why don't you just ask her out?" she inquired. Having

your mom around you all day, every day, doesn't make for the most private love life.

"You can't be serious. Who would want to go out with me?"

"Well, she's always around, so she must like something about you."

"Mom, I can't feel anything from the collarbone down. What could I possibly do for her?"

"What's the worst that could happen? If you never ask a girl out, you'll never get a date." She had a point.

After perfecting the art of the transfer, I familiarized myself with the hands-only operation of my van. Weird, but workable. The first drive I took was from my house to Nicole's. The doorways to her house weren't wheelchair accessible so we just relaxed outside. Tom was glad I brought my bike, and I was glad I had cleared another hurdle and gained an inch of independence back.

As Nicole's custody battle moved along, I thought more about what my mom said. Then my friend Terry came to Dufur for a visit with his girlfriend. We all went on a ride through Mt. Hood National Forest—I drove—and I decided that I would ask Nicole out that very night. We went back to my house and I waited for Terry to leave. And I waited. And waited. When he finally got up to go, Nicole decided she'd head home at the same time. Wonderful. I said goodbye to both of them as they drove off in their cars.

Plans foiled, I was still pretty wound up. So I sat outside, watched the stars plod across the sky and contemplated the situation. Ten o'clock rolled around and I decided to call Nicole.

I stuttered and stammered through my question. It wasn't anything special or romantic. I basically just asked her, "Be my girlfriend?" All my chips were in and I was waiting for that final turn of the card.

"Yes," is all I remembered her saying.

I hadn't felt more alive since my accident. I was dating someone! Officially dating someone! The guy who can't feel below his collarbone has a girlfriend! I wanted to yell it out across the hills of Dufur. But I didn't.

As happy as I was, it was a little difficult to cuddle. Actually, it wasn't the Chair or the paralysis that got in the way. I lived at home. She lived at home. On top of navigating the parental units, Tom was around to keep tabs on me. Nicole and I would be cuddling on my bed, snuggled under a comforter watching a movie, and every once in a while Tom would look up from his Hot Wheels and give me a dirty look. It was like we were in junior high again, only it was more complicated.

At the end of September, things really started to seem like junior high. Nicole left for a two-week trip to California. It was hard, her being away, but we had been talking about long-distance relationships and I thought of it as a trial. How well we managed to be apart in those two weeks would show me how well we would do if she took a temporary job in Germany, as she planned to do.

Those two weeks did not go well. Our lines of

communication were shut down. I went from constant contact to two texts and zero calls from her in those two long weeks. I was a mess.

When she got back to Dufur, something had changed. She couldn't see me, even though she lived down the road. She had a headache. She felt sick.

Man, I thought, this is dumb.

Before she left for another week-long trip, I called her and told her that it wasn't working out. Other than agreeing, she didn't say much. Later that month she and Tom boarded a plane for Europe.

It wasn't the most romantic relationship. As fun and exciting as Nicole was, ending it when I realized it wasn't going to work out was hard. But it was also positive because, in those two months, I found what I'd been glimpsing since my injury: my old self. I stopped thinking about all the things that weren't "possible" any more. I had concluded that getting an attractive girl to date me was impossible, yet it happened. My own expectations of what my life could be had been limiting my life. I decided I wouldn't let that happen any longer. In the words of the immortal Dr. Seuss, whose works I love, "Don't cry because it's over, smile because it happened."

It was time to do a little living.

One of my goals was to get outside again and enjoy the wonderful outdoors. I used to be a good shot, but how could I possibly hit a target as a quadriplegic? Basically, I had to train myself to shoot again. Frustrating? Well, let's say that using just two fingers to shoot a weapon makes for some interesting target practice, and I had the bruises on my chest to prove it! However, my brother Brad created the most ingenious table to enable me to rest my gun on a bipod; the table hooks onto my chair. The rewards of the retraining were worth the hours of practice. I'd soon be able to use my shooting abilities.

Matt Blewett, a wonderful friend from college, and his brother Luke helped me accomplish my goals. Matt's brother Luke, ranch manager at the Heartland Wildlife Ranches in Ethel, Missouri, arranged for Heartland to donate a hunt so that I could test my new skills. The gift included a hunt for me as well as gourmet meals and exquisite accommodations for five. It also meant that I would make my maiden flight as a quad. Southwest Airlines couldn't have been more terrific in helping me feel comfortable, and the trip only got better when I shot a red stag! My friends even paid for the taxidermy. Not only was it a vacation I'll never forget, but also it was an amazing confidence-building experience on many levels.

My mom and I found out about Project Walk, a nonprofit 501(c)(3) therapy facility in Carlsbad, California. The Project Walk staff focuses on getting severely paralyzed folks like me out of their wheelchairs both as a goal and as a method of treatment, an outside-the-box approach. They found that by focusing on exercises that shun the wheelchair, the body starts to connect in surprising ways. At their facility, quads who have never thought they would walk again have taken their first steps since their injuries. There was just one problem: After the expenses at the hospital, the cost of the remodel and buying a new wheelchair-accessible van, we didn't have enough money to make more than one trip to Project Walk.

I shared my personal story and hopes about Project Walk with Clackamas County Sheriff Craig Roberts, who took my cause to the Clackamas County Peace Officers' Benevolent Foundation. They helped raise money for a therapeutic trip to California, which my mom and I took in November almost a year after my injury. During one of the sessions there, I actually felt tingling in my legs for the first time since my injury. I'm not saying I was healed or that it was a miracle but, with a paralyzing injury, I've learned that progress is all about small victories.

In the spring of 2010, we found a facility in Beaverton, Oregon, named ADAPT Advanced. Its neuromuscular redevelopment program has similar goals as Project Walk and, because of its proximity to family members, my mom and I have no lodging expenses.

The biggest victory didn't have anything to do with my paralysis. During a conversation, I was trying to explain my thoughts on letting go of the past and moving forward with a positive attitude when I said, "Life happens. Live it."

My mom stopped me. She repeated it. "Life happens. Live it?"

"Sure!" I said. I wasn't as poetic as Shakespeare, but those two short sentences summed up my ideas perfectly.

"Jake," she said, "you need to tell people about this."

Life Happens—Live It

My life to date reminds me of a bamboo plant. According to a Chinese parable, planting a bamboo seed in the ground takes patience as the planter must wait for it to germinate and grow. Year after year, nothing happens. Is the seed bad, the dirt not rich enough or the rainfall insufficient? Around the fifth year, the plant sprouts and begins to grow at an amazing rate. All of the growth in the first four years is underground as the plant builds a deep root structure. It must have solid footing in order to break ground and shoot skyward.

It took me a lifetime to get to where I am today, and now I'm growing by leaps and bounds in so many ways. I can hold myself up in my wheelchair, feed myself, drive a car, write a book and share my story with audiences everywhere as a public speaker. My history of being the king of preparation continues to serve me well in my new life, as does my pragmatic nature.

I could say that my public speaking career began when my mom repeated those four words back to me, but that's too much of a Hallmark moment. My new career really began when I thought my life had ended. Since that day in the mini-mart parking lot, I've been progressing toward this career. First, I had to realize that life doesn't make me happy; I make myself happy. My happiness doesn't depend on my ability to tie a fishing line, walk or date. Lots of people who can do all those things are perfectly miserable.

What are the important lessons I've learned?

Each of us decides if we will live a life that matters. It's a choice. Like all living things, you and I will die. There will be no more years, months, weeks, days, hours, minutes or even seconds left to choose how we live. Living a life that matters doesn't happen by accident; it happens each and every day as a result of the decisions you make.

I make a choice every day about how to live this life I've been given. It's *my* life, and I choose what my limitations will be. I didn't choose to have my neck broken that night in Eagle Creek. I didn't choose to live life in a wheelchair. But I have decided that I am going to take life standing up, whether I'm standing up or not.

Happiness to me is a simple thing. It is something I choose to be. I'm a simple guy who wanted a simple life, and I'm fortunate that I have a simple message which I hope to share with millions. When I look into the eyes of my audience members as I speak, I can see that they understand exactly what I mean. Yet, it's not easy for everyone to put into play the lessons I've learned. Some in the audience may feel sorry for me because I'm wheelchair bound, but I consider myself one of the lucky ones because I love my life and make the most of it each day.

I ask you to perform this easy task: Look in the mirror each morning and ask yourself, "Will I make the most of this day by having a positive attitude? Will I choose to make myself happy today?" Your answers are the keys to living your best life.

I close each of my speeches with this Dr. Seuss quote:

You have brains in your head.

You have feet in your shoes.

You can steer yourself in any direction

you choose.

You're on your own

And you know what you know.

And YOU are the guy who'll decide where to go.

As for me, I'm moving forward. Life happens. Live it.

Source Material

Amazon.com. *Oh, the Places You'll Go!* Dr. Seuss. Random House, 1990. www.amazon.com.

Dufur School District #29. "Scholarship: Jerri Walker DePriest Memorial Endowment Fund." www.dufur.k12.or.us.

Goodreads.com. "Dr. Seuss quotes." www.goodreads.com.

Holisticonline.com. "Pet Therapy." www.holisticonline.com.

Massachusetts Institutes of Technology. "Oh, the Places You'll Go! by Dr. Suess." www.mit.edu.

Mike Wills Learning Services. "Anecdotes and Fables." www.mwls.co.uk.

National Speakers Association-Illinois. "Michael Schwass." www.nsa-il.org.

University of Idaho. "Logger Sports Club." www.cnrhome.uidaho.edu.

Wizdompath. "An Old Cherokee Tale of Two Wolves." wizdompath.wordpress.com.

The Heart of a Lioness
The Arielle Rausin Story

The wheels spin across an oval track baked brown in the hot sun. The racers grunt and grimace, faces sweating in the relentless heat. Cheers from the crowd fill their ears and add to the adrenaline coursing through their muscles. Once more hurtling toward a turn, the competitors gauge their speed and the speed of those they pursue. They can hear one another sucking oxygen, despite the noise of the wheels on clay and the crowd. Speed is their motto.

Despite some similarities, these chariot drivers are not at Circus Maximus and don't rely on horses. These are adaptive athletes racing in a sport that is a mixture of physical performance and modern engineering. Arielle Rausin, one of the adaptive athletes, is trying to race her way to the 2012 Paralympics in London. Yet up until 2009, Arielle's home state of Florida didn't officially recognize adapted track. With the heart of a Roman champion, Arielle and her family have fought a pitched bureaucratic battle for recognition.

Don't let her perpetual laughter or the mischievous twinkle in her eyes fool you. With her sandy blond hair and powerfully built shoulders, Arielle's bearing is more lioness than jester, which doesn't surprise Krista Rausin, Arielle's mom. She still remembers learning the meaning of Arielle's name when she was pregnant with her: *Lion of God.* It is a name worthy of a gladiator.

This lioness' story started when she was a just a cub during a Thanksgiving weekend in 2003.

I Want to Go Home

Krista Rausin felt a buzz of nervous tension race along her nerves as she took her seat on the plane. Her husband, Eric, was calmly sitting next to her. The software company Eric worked for was sending executives and their spouses to the Gulf Coast of Mexico for the long Thanksgiving weekend. It was supposed to be a chance for employees and their significant others to mix a little business with a lot of fun. Hijinks and bonding were practically a foregone conclusion. But Krista didn't feel like celebrating. With Arielle and Kai, her two young children, at their grandparents' house, it was going to be an unusual Thanksgiving weekend.

Arielle was an extremely bright ten-year-old who could already play the piano and violin. She loved being around friends and family, especially her grandparents Marilyn and Joe Dondero and their youngest daughter Michelle. Technically Michelle was Arielle's aunt, but the two were close enough in age that they treated one another like cousins.

While Krista was excited about the long, romantic weekend she would be spending with her husband, she felt an emptiness in the pit of her stomach. After ten years of motherhood, she was used to the feeling of low-grade anxiety. Not wanting her kids to experience the same worry, she and Eric had devised a way to keep their children's spirits up during their first extended weekend away from their parents. Eric and Krista had placed surprises in the children's luggage: a small present for each of them for every day the family was separated. The rule was that they could open one present each day their parents were gone. When they ran out of presents, the kids knew they would be seeing their parents soon.

Thanksgiving Day in Mexico was an unusual one for Krista. Watching the traditional holiday parade was replaced with jet skiing on the placid waters of the Gulf. Instead of touch football, Eric joined a game of beach volleyball. Watching him set, serve and spike reminded Krista of the beaches of California and their early years together. She began dating Eric while they were both living in California; while watching him play, she realized he hadn't touched a volleyball since they'd moved to Florida.

After margaritas at the poolside bar and a shower, Krista donned a light summer dress and joined a spiffed-up Eric for some moonlit dancing. It felt less like Thanksgiving and more like a honeymoon to Krista. It was after midnight when they finally collapsed into bed, exhausted but finally relaxed.

Thanksgiving weekend was an unusual one for Kai and Arielle as well. Though spending time with the Donderos was typical for most holidays, this year things were a little different.

They were going to be having dinner at a family friend's house near Clermont, northeast of Tampa and perfectly centered between Florida's two coasts. Arielle missed her parents but it was fun hanging out with Michelle. When it came time to load up the car for the trip out to Clermont, Arielle and Michelle wanted to sit next to each other so Michelle could braid Arielle's hair. Kai didn't need to be asked twice. He had the bad luck to be both the smallest and the minority so he was typically stuck between the girls in the middle seat.

It was a long drive to Clermont from Orlando, and soon the hair was braided and the three kids began getting antsy. To distract the kids, Marilyn and Joe started a contest to see which child could guess the exact time they would arrive at their destination.

Then Joe missed the turn off the highway to the house. When he had a chance to turn around, he pulled into the left turn lane and waited for traffic to clear.

Krista Rausin awoke at three in the morning with the phone filling her ears with its shrill ringing. With her mind still somewhere in dreamland, Krista's hand picked up the phone and she heard strange voices. Was it Eric's friends, still up, deciding to play some pranks using the hotel phones? Her hand started to replace the phone in the base. Her mind would be able to find dreamland again before the line disconnected. Then she heard a stranger's voice.

"Is this Krista Rausin?" Krista froze.

"Yes," she said.

"Please hold," came the reply.

When Krista heard her father's voice, her heart began to race.

"Krista, there's been an accident. We need you to come home. Kai's okay; your mom is in the hospital," he paused. "We are worried about Arielle."

Krista's body went numb. All she could hear was her heart beating and her dad's slow breathing. Was her baby girl being taken from her? This couldn't be happening. She kept telling herself to wake up. They had just celebrated her baby girl's birthday. Just ten years old, Krista wasn't ready to say goodbye yet.

Her dad broke the silence. "Arielle has a bruise on her spinal cord and she's unable to move her legs." Oh. A bruise. It's just a bruise. She's okay.

"We're coming home," Krista said and hung up the phone. Eric was awake, listening to the end of what sounded like a bizarre and troubling conversation. When Krista relayed to him the little information she had, he was beside himself. They both felt like the world had turned upside down.

Discovering that there were no flights out of Mexico for four hours, the Rausins were trapped, powerless to do anything but wait and worry. Hours later and they were finally by Arielle's side, trying to get answers and calm the scared ten-year-old.

"I want to go home," Arielle kept telling her mom. But they couldn't leave the hospital. The doctors kept telling the

Rausins that Arielle's bruised spinal cord was causing the lower-body paralysis. To Krista and Eric, this bruise sounded like a temporary thing. In actuality, Arielle had suffered a T-11 injury to the lower thoracic region of her spinal cord. Still, they couldn't get a definitive prognosis from the doctors. For two weeks they waited for the experts to decide about Arielle's chances to overcome the paralysis. The examinations were frequent at first, then became less frequent.

As the testing decreased, Krista started hearing the word "rehab" more frequently. It sounded like a place where Arielle would be able to recover. The social worker at the hospital had even fewer answers than the medical experts. The confusion about Arielle's condition was terribly frustrating. To add to the Rausins' uneasiness, the hospital allowed sales staff from the different rehabilitation facilities access to the troubled parents. Krista and Eric wanted what was best for their daughter, so they sat through one sales pitch after another, but they still struggled to make decisions about Arielle's future. Parenthood doesn't come with a manual, but Eric and Krista didn't expect one. They had family and friends who had done it all before them, but this was new. No one they knew and no one at the hospital could help them with the life-changing decisions they were now faced with making.

When they heard about a facility in Atlanta that sounded perfect, they found out that their insurance wouldn't cover much, if any, of the cost. Just to get Arielle started would require an up-front payment of $10,000 from the Rausins. Then an acquaintance recommended a facility in Miami. Finally, it felt like they were going to take a step toward getting their lives back. From the hospital in Orlando, Arielle went to the rehabilitation facility in Miami. It wasn't home, but at least there was forward momentum.

The facility was horrendous. It housed prison inmates in the floors above the children's wing. Conditions were so dirty that Arielle contracted ringworm. Recalling the dirt and smell of the place still causes her mom to cringe. Every week Eric and Krista traded between Cape Coral and Miami in order for Arielle always to have a parent with her. It wasn't an ideal situation but, for the three weeks Arielle was in Miami, it worked.

Arielle was still at the rehabilitation facility during Christmas. The Rausins didn't have the ability to get her home and were considering the possibility of celebrating Christmas in Miami. A Fort Myers-based medical transport service stepped up and generously provided a ride for Arielle and Krista to Coral Gables on Christmas Day. All of the Rausins' friends and family were present. Although many of them had already been to the Orlando or Miami medical facilities to see Arielle, this was the first time Arielle had been home since Thanksgiving. It was an emotional day which, unfortunately, had to end with the three-hour trip back to Miami.

As her mom and dad worried about Arielle's future and what kind of life she would be forced to lead because of her paralysis, the ten-year-old lived in the present. She and her parents learned all the Miami rehab facility had to teach in three weeks. When the human body is paralyzed from the waist down, some bodily functions have to be done manually, which can become a source of anxiety and embarrassment. When Arielle seemed to take these inconvenient and sometimes humiliating chores in stride, she proved once again what a special kid she was.

Arielle had always been a great kid. Her parents couldn't have asked for a smarter, funnier and more caring ten-year-old. After the car accident, her family saw the cub turning into the lioness. As she dealt with the hard situation she found herself in, Arielle started to display the heart of a conqueror.

In 49 BC another conqueror, this one named Caesar, paused at the banks of a river called the Rubicon. Crossing the river with his army and entering his home country meant war. As Krista drove Arielle toward home, they crossed the bridge into Cape Coral. Arielle was returning home and, like Caesar, this was the point of no return where she could no longer turn back. The old life was behind them. Ahead would be struggles, battles and maybe victories. The little girl who looked out the window at Fort Myers wasn't a Roman general fond of laurel wreaths. As her family has since learned, however, Caesar's motto of *veni, vidi, vici* could be her own. When it comes to arriving, seeing what she wants and getting it, Arielle's spirit is just as tenacious as Caesar's.

Just back from her stay at the rehabilitation hospital, Arielle decided to jump back into school. Edison Park Elementary, where Arielle attended school and her mom taught, was renowned for its academic standards. She knew that getting back to her schoolwork and friends would be the first step in getting her life back. Again, she approached the problem head-on. Some odd looks greeted her, but her good friends had already seen her and accepted her new "accessories." Still, the stress was building. Arielle made it through most of her first day without any accidents. Having her mom there helped. In fact, the support from everyone at the school, from the principal on down, was terrific.

Halfway through the day, the stress became too much. Everything was the same, but everything was experienced anew. Her perspective on life was knocked out of alignment and the cognitive dissonance was starting to affect her stomach. Recess was different. The bathrooms were different. Not feeling well, she asked if she could go to the bathroom. Her first day back, she found herself in the bathroom trying to figure out the best way to throw up into the toilet without getting it on her wheelchair.

Afterward, when she got back to class, Arielle didn't feel as bad. Her perspective might never return to so-called normal, but like all the other changes, she would gradually get used to her new life.

Krista wasn't surprised that Arielle had gotten sick on her first day. She felt her own anxiety stretch her nerves to the breaking point. With the anxiety, however, she also felt a mother's pride as she watched her daughter make it through the day without breaking down mentally. Her stomach might have revolted against her iron will, but Arielle didn't let that stop her. She went back to class and kept going back to class until she left for junior high at North Fort Myers Academy for the Arts.

Though Arielle was adjusting well to life in a wheelchair, her parents worried that they weren't doing enough to make her better. Therapy was—and still is—their only option. Arielle saw some physical therapists in Fort Myers but she was usually finished with their rehabilitation regimen ahead of schedule. This is, after all, the ten-year-old who learned how to self-catheter so she could go hang out with friends. The Rausins were going to have to look outside Fort Myers for a challenge to match Arielle's ability. Hopefully, by rising to meet the challenge, they would see more concrete results in Arielle's ability to use her legs. Eric and Krista were also worried about regret. They didn't want Arielle looking back with bitterness and asking them why they didn't explore every avenue of treatment.

The best therapy program the Rausins found was the Rehabilitation Institute of Michigan (RIM) located in Detroit. They decided to give it a chance. Because they didn't have jobs in Detroit, the Rausins rented an apartment twenty minutes from RIM's facility. The therapy started in March 2004, so Arielle had to leave her sixth grade friends at Fort Myers Academy before the end of the school year. Eric was able to do some of his work remotely; from March to May, he stayed in Detroit with Arielle. Krista's boss, Principal Charlotte Rafferty, was incredibly supportive throughout Arielle's recovery and let Krista leave for summer break early. Enabling Krista to join Arielle in May meant that Eric could return to Florida. Kai bounced not only between Krista and Eric but also between Detroit and Florida.

The Rausins had adopted a semi-nomadic lifestyle. They pulled Arielle from her sixth grade year and diligently attended therapy sessions three times a week hoping that Arielle's condition would improve. The logistics were only part of the challenge. Even if Arielle regained some use of her legs, Eric and Krista wondered if they were making the right decision. Arielle wouldn't let her physical abilities define her. Her social life in Florida was a huge part of what made her happy. Arielle needed to be a kid. The patients at RIM were typically adults and, though they formed a friendly, supportive community, they weren't going to have the same relationship as her best forever friends at school. It didn't help that the Rausins weren't seeing the improvements they had hoped to see.

Eric and Krista discussed how things were going and the life experiences Arielle was missing while she was in Detroit. They were still worried that if they left RIM they might be giving up on Arielle's eventual recovery. Yet, they also wondered if pushing Arielle toward recovery was sending her the message that they wouldn't love her unless she could walk again. More than anything else, they wanted Arielle to know that they would love, accept and support her whether or not she was in a wheelchair.

Krista and Eric also wanted Arielle to know they respected her, so they sat down and simply asked her what she would rather do. They could stay in Detroit. Years of therapy loomed ahead with no guarantee of recovery. Or, they could move back to Florida. Arielle would be back in school hanging out with her friends, but she might be using a wheelchair for the rest of her life.

Arielle chose Florida. She went home and stayed home.

Life in the Fast Lane

The Rausins moved back to Florida in mid-July and Arielle had the rest of the summer to adjust and be with her friends. As Arielle started school in the fall, she was excited about taking PE even though Krista wasn't sure it was such a good idea. That's where Arielle met Coach Black. Coach Black saw Arielle as a kid who was looking for a challenge. Like all great mentors, she made sure she set the bar for Arielle just out of her reach. It didn't matter that Arielle was in a wheelchair and unable to do certain things. She could do plenty, and using the wheelchair itself turned into a challenge. Like all great mentors, Coach Black gave Arielle the support she needed to meet her goals.

Coach Black's inspiration led to Arielle's interest in track. It was the perfect fit. Wheelchairs, after all, are made to roll, and propelling a wheelchair around a track as fast as she could spin the wheels was fun. It was also challenging, both physically and mentally.

Arielle's interest in track came at a perfect time. Eric was getting interested in running in a local 5k race and Krista found herself constantly busy with teaching duties at Edison Park. Then one day Arielle came home and told her parents that she wouldn't be able to join her school's track team because she was in a wheelchair. Even Coach Black's hands were tied. It was an administrative regulation which couldn't be overruled at the school level. Krista told Arielle she'd talk to her boss, Principal Rafferty, about whom to contact about making an exception.

A week had past and still Krista hadn't heard from anyone at the school-district administration level. She was on her way to work in the morning when the radio personality she had been listening to started telling his audience about a paralyzed middle-school student at North Fort Myers Academy for the Arts who wasn't allowed to join the track team.

Krista turned up the volume. He had to be talking about Arielle—no other kids at her school in wheelchairs were trying to join the track team. He invited callers to give their opinions about whether or not the student should be allowed on the team. Already upset, Krista started getting angry while she listened to a caller give a close-minded opinion about why Arielle shouldn't be allowed on the team. By the time Krista got to Edison Park, she was so mad she was shaking.

Krista learned that another student's mom had started a petition on Arielle's behalf at Fort Myers Academy. Somehow the radio station had found out and decided to ask its listeners for their opinions on the matter. The school district was going to think that Krista had started the petition on Arielle's behalf. Once Krista had found out what had happened, she went to see her boss. Principal Rafferty, who had been wonderful to Arielle and Krista throughout the year, deserved an explanation.

Krista was summoned from class to take a call in the office from the superintendent of the district. He wanted to know why Krista hadn't used official channels. She tried explaining that she was just as mad and just as surprised as he was; he kept telling her that if she needed help with Arielle's access to school programs, she should have come to him.

Though the surprise petition got Krista into hot water at work, the attention it garnered changed the school's policy about letting Arielle race. The focus was good for Arielle, both physically and mentally. Eric, whose interest in jogging inspired his daughter, ran with Arielle in her first 5K in February of 2007. A few more 5Ks and the father-daughter team was ready for Disney's Race for the Taste 10K in October that year. As Arielle crossed the finish line in her daily-use wheelchair, the announcer applauded the seventh-grader's accomplishment and pointed out that someone needed to get her a racing chair. Krista, welcoming her two athletes with cold water bottles in hand, heard the announcer as her eyes met Eric's eyes. *Racing wheelchair?*

The finish-line announcer wasn't the only one who noticed Arielle's commitment to racing. In the crowd was a representative from the Challenged Athletes Foundation (CAF).

The CAF helps people with physical disabilities get involved in sports so they can pursue healthy, active lifestyles. Grandfather Joe Dondero also noticed a budding track star in the race. After a contribution from the Donderos, the CAF found Arielle a custom-fit racing chair. Three months later Arielle raced in Tampa's Gasparilla 15k. Her new, lightweight chair carved off an hour from her time. Still in seventh grade, Arielle was stacking up an impressive racing resume.

Before Arielle started high school, her mom realized two things: Arielle's wheelchair racing was not a fad, and her own teaching career was taking up so much of her time that she had been unable to fully participate in Arielle's early struggles and enjoy her successes in racing. She didn't know if their family could survive on just one person's income; she knew that if she kept working, she would miss more and more of her daughter's life. In the end, it wasn't a hard decision. Following her resignation, however, their finances were precarious for a little while.

As a freshman at North Fort Myers High School, Arielle had her own struggles. When she went out for the track team, she learned from the coach that, though she would be allowed to practice with the team, she couldn't travel with them to their meets. It was the middle-school dilemma all over again. This time her mom wasn't working for the school district, so Krista had some time on her hands. Mom decided to get involved.

Championing for a Champion

The State of Florida wasn't quite ready for adaptive sports when Arielle started ninth grade. Arielle was ready, however, and she was going to race her wheelchair. She either won over those who stood in her way or she went around them. It was still frustrating for the Rausins, who made their case for Arielle's right to use the facilities and take advantage of the coach's expertise just like any other student at the school. With her goal set on the 2012 Paralympics in London, Arielle knew that simply racing around the high school track by herself wasn't enough to ensure that she would get there. Arielle's mom and dad couldn't have been more supportive, but Arielle needed to find a mentor who knew the science of competition.

Because of the rules written by the Florida High School Athletic Association (FHSAA), Arielle wasn't technically allowed on the team or to wear her school's jersey. Yet she discovered a mentor in Coach Purish. For the first time in all the years she had coached track, Coach Purish found herself in a professional dilemma. She had a dedicated student who just wanted to race, but regulations disqualified the ambitious girl from racing for her school. Still, Coach Purish worked to develop Arielle's talent by finding some space between the rules. Arielle raced over twenty miles a week; when she wasn't racing, she lifted weights. Coach Purish found the fastest adaptive track times in Arielle's region and made her race against them. The problem: Arielle was racing against her own best times.

Arielle was in athletic limbo. She was allowed on the team because school officials knew that not letting her on the team looked discriminatory. But her ability to race at actual meets was at the discretion of the school hosting the event. Krista started a school-by-school campaign to get Arielle permission to participate in future meets, even though she only was allowed to race against her own times.

Doing what she loved with the benefit of a coach was better than racing by herself on the track after hours. Even if she just tried to beat her own time, Arielle loved the new experience of getting cheered on by students and parents attending the meet. In March 2009 Arielle was allowed to race in an open mile during a track meet at Charlotte High School. Krista was able to watch her daughter, after a slow start, beat all but one other girl to the finish line. As well as Arielle performed at the meets, without any official status she wasn't able to earn points for her team. Racing in her school's uniform, she still felt like an outsider when she was unable to contribute points to the team like its other members.

Arielle had her sights set on higher goals. The guidance Arielle received from Coach Purish helped her prepare for the Emory Invitational High School and Collegiate Wheelchair Track & Field Meet in Atlanta, Georgia, held two weeks after the Charlotte meet. Hosted by Emory University's School of Medicine's Division of Physical Therapy and the American Association of Adapted Sports Programs, the event was another step on Arielle's journey to the London Paralympics and a chance to show what she'd learned on the track team.

During her first year of track at North Fort Myers high school, Arielle was essentially the team mascot. Off the packed clay, she was hilarious and fun to be around. She inspired her teammates to be faster and take life's challenges in stride. On the track her intense drive was contagious but, because her ability to compete was at the discretion of so many parties, Arielle was never really a full-fledged member of the track team. It was time for that to change.

The catalyst for the change could have been the letter Krista received from the staff of a leadership camp. In the process of trying to persuade them to allow Arielle to attend without her, Krista received a liability waiver. In part it stated that if the camp, in its sole discretion,

> decides that Arielle is unable to participate in Tour activities, and/or has interfered with the experience or enjoyment of any other participant or attendee of the Tour due to her inability to participate in Tour activities or otherwise, Arielle will be immediately sent home at her family's expense.

Using the guise of a potential liability problem, the camp was attempting to discriminate against Arielle. It wasn't likely that they sent the same waiver to the rest of the camp attendees; nor was it likely that, if another student interfered with Arielle's enjoyment, the staff would send the other camper home at the expense of that camper's family.

The waiver crystallized the track issue for the Rausins. Krista began petitioning the FHSAA for the right for adaptive athletes to compete statewide in athletic competitions. As with any change, traditionalists pushed back, but Arielle's cause was aided by two dedicated advocates. Lewis Friedland, from the CAF, met with the FHSAA while it was considering changing the rules to include adapted track. The most powerful advocate was the FHSAA's own Executive Director, Dr. Roger Dearing. Like Arielle, his daughter was paralyzed as the result of a car accident and uses a wheelchair. Her disability opened his eyes to the reality of what racing means to adaptive athletes like Arielle. Dr. Dearing saw that the opportunities which could result from a regulation change far outweighed any bureaucratic hassles necessary to make the change happen.

The FHSAA board passed the proposal to allow adaptive athletes the same rights to compete in high school track. On May 7th, 2010, Arielle raced in the state track meet, competing in all three adapted track and field events.

During the summer of 2010, Arielle attended the University of Illinois' Adapted Athletics summer camp put on by the school's Disability Resources and Educational Services. After the camp, Arielle raced in the National Junior Disability Championships in Lake Forest, Illinois, in preparation for the London Paralympics.

A Life Inspirational

Arielle Rausin's dreams are bigger than track. Because the "what happened to you" question is a common yet sometimes inconsiderate query when asked by complete strangers, Arielle is fond of making up outrageously convoluted stories. It isn't surprising that she found out she has a gift for the theater through the North Fort Myers High School drama department. Not one to let a newfound gift go ignored, the Rausins sent Arielle to film camp during the summer of 2009 where she made two short films. She continues to look for video projects—when she's not racing, that is.

Track is still a perfect outlet for Arielle's competitive spirit. She needs a way to channel both her drive for success and the daily frustrations she faces. So she races. She creates. And she inspires.

Even without track, Arielle's days are full of challenges which by themselves seem almost Herculean. Yet she takes Advanced Placement courses and gets straight A's. She plays in the band and performs in musical theater. And before she's done with her day, she's out on the track, speeding along, propelled by her muscles alone. Inspiring others is a byproduct of her life and isn't something that she thinks much about. She likes to think of herself as a regular kid with typical issues living a typical life. Even in her ability to be regular, heroism surfaces.

One person touched by Arielle's life created a list of

what Arielle inspires others to do:

> Honor people for whom they truly are. Don't
> expect them to be just like you.
> Smiling opens doors that would otherwise be closed.
> A light within illuminates with praise and
> encouragement.
> When life shocks you, be brave.
> Don't cry for what you have lost; ask yourself how to
> use what you have.

By conquering her disability, the heart of this lioness has conquered the hearts of others, including mine.

Source Material

"Adaptive Track and Field" on YouTube.
www.youtube.com/watch?v=xECigGyYhuQ&feature=player_embedded#!

Challenged Athletes Foundation. CAF Mission Statement.
www.challengedathletes.org.

Fortier, Michel. "Our World: Like a champion." *Naples Daily News*. Sunday, August 17, 2008. www.naplesnews.com.

Gerth, Rob. "Wouldn't you want Elle at your leadership camp?" The Daily Dose. Christopher & Dana Reeve Foundation. May 06, 2009. www.communities.kintera.org.

Rausin, Krista. "Lessons From My Daughter." September 16, 2008. http://kdrausin.wordpress.com.

———— "Standing Up for What Is Right." Christopher & Dana Reeve Foundation (C&DRF). www.christopherreeve.org.

Tampa Bay Online. "FHSAA considering track events for wheelchair athletes." September 28, 2009. www2.tbo.com.

Never Give Up!

The Ron Heagy Story

Nothing thrilled Ron Heagy more than adventure. When he was a teenager, he loved riding up the side of a mountain on a motorcycle with the throttle held open. He was the starting fullback on his high school's varsity football team. He loved the thrill of pinning his opponents during wrestling matches. If it was wild, crazy or a journey into the unknown, Ron Heagy enthusiastically signed up.

During the spring break of his senior year, Ron planned his biggest adventure of all. Alone in his VW bug, he would drive from Brownsville, Oregon, to Huntington Beach, California, on the open road for a week of surfing, swimming and hanging out with beach babes. Well, he almost made the trip alone. His mom, Terry, pulled Ron aside just before he left and persuaded him to take Mike, his thirteen-year-old brother, with him. Thank goodness his sister Pennie wasn't interested in making the trip or his mother would have insisted she tag along, too.

The two teenagers headed south for what Ron hoped would be a memorable spring vacation.

It was a vacation that changed his life.

A Leap of Fate

Ron looked back at the beach where Mike lay with their friend Justin. The two seemed content to simply lie there, soaking up rays. But for Ron this was no time to tan or lie around. He could lie around in Oregon. It was adventure time.

Ron walked toward the shoreline and dipped his feet in the ocean. As the icy cold water numbed his toes, the beach blanket started to look appealing to Ron. He watched a swell move toward shore, gaining momentum as it approached. What the heck, he thought. You only live once. He waited until the wave crested. Then, with a running start, Ron sprinted through the shallow surf and dove head first into the breaker.

Tons of churning water rushed over him as his dive propelled him forward beneath the surf, straight toward a hidden sand bar.

His head hit the wall of sand. He felt a crunching sensation and heard a loud crack as his head snapped backward. His head bent so far that the back of it struck him between his shoulder blades. His body went numb except for the excruciating pain knifing up from his neck.

The wave swirled on, carrying him with it. The downward surge pushed Ron into the sand, scraping his face across the shell-strewn bottom. He needed air *fast*. Trying to get to the surface, Ron kicked, but his legs wouldn't move. It felt like a nightmare, but this was no dream. He tried pushing himself off the sand with his arms, but his arms wouldn't work. The water reversed direction and started pulling him away from the beach.

In desperate need of air, he could see sunlight on the water's surface, but he wasn't able to reach it. He finally realized what was going on. He was drowning.

He prayed that God would help him live.

God helped him, but in His own way.

After Ron trotted off toward the water, Mike rolled over and closed his eyes. Then he raised his head to watch Ron take the plunge. He saw Ron's arms go up as he put his elbows next to his ears, then he saw Ron's head go under the wave, his wet back glistening in the sun. He kept watching.

As he saw Ron's body flip in a quick somersault, uneasiness came over Mike. He watched the surf, waiting for Ron's head to reappear.

Something is wrong, Mike realized.

No one was in the water. No swimmers, no surfers. Without a word to Justin, Mike began running toward the water before he even knew why.

"Ron!"

He had seen only a flash of color as one small wave rose, then broke—just a dot of dark blue that was quickly swallowed up by the churning water.

Bouncing his helpless body off the bottom, the undertow was rolling Ron like a barrel, a flailing tangle of arms and legs being swept out to sea.

"Ron! Ron! Where are you?" Mike screamed. Running through the shallows, he suddenly dropped into water over his head as the bottom fell away. He was frantically treading water, fighting the tide to stay in the spot where he'd seen Ron pop up a moment before. Sucking in a deep breath of air, he plunged under the surface, anxiously trying to see through the froth and bubbles.

Nothing.

He resurfaced and struggled to see but was blocked by the swell of the waves. He sucked in a quick breath and dove again.

Nothing.

Mike swam, not knowing which way to go, but he instinctively headed into deeper water.

"Ron!" he kept calling.

He dove once more and caught a glimpse of Ron, eerily tumbling as if in slow motion as the current pulled his body away from his younger brother. Mike plunged down again, pressing his feet to the sandy bottom as he aligned himself under Ron and pushed upward.

Ron was fighting his own battle, hoping, praying and holding his breath while tumbling through the surf. Finally, with his lungs on fire, he resigned himself to the inevitable. He sucked in, expecting salt water to fill his lungs. Instead, his lungs filled with fresh ocean air.

A pair of scrawny arms was tightly wrapped around Ron, although he couldn't feel them at the time. It was Mike! But he was losing the struggle to hold Ron's head above water. The thirteen-year-old didn't have the strength to keep his much larger brother's head above the waves.

Ron gulped in a great gasp of salty air, opened his eyes and glimpsed the sun before his head once again slid below the surface.

Ron sank, his eyes desperately searching through the ascending bubbles to make sense of what was happening. A body streaked down through the water beside him, and once again Ron rocketed upward, his head breaking the surface and his lungs once again drawing in the sweet air.

But as Ron sank again, he realized that it was just too much work for his brother to do.

"Mike!" Ron cried out a moment later when his head once again broke the surface. "Go back, Mike!"

"No, Ron!" Mike stubbornly shot back. "I can't let you drown!"

Ron tried forcing Mike away, hoping his little brother would see the logic in his sacrifice, but Ron couldn't move his arms.

They were in water that fluctuated from twelve to fifteen feet depending on the swells. Mike tried holding on to Ron while treading water and catching his breath, but Ron was just too heavy, even with the added buoyancy of the salt water. Again and again they sank to the bottom, and again and again Mike pushed off with his feet. As he propelled them upward, he angled them toward the shore, like a dolphin pushing a ball.

Mike finally got Ron to shallow water. Ron looked at his arms and legs. They seemed detached from his body, each one floating in a different direction. By now the two boys were both exhausted, and Ron was having a hard time breathing.

At Ron's urging, Mike tried holding him in a sitting position to help him breathe, but it didn't help. Ron's head flopped from side to side. Mike laid Ron back down. As the trauma and exhaustion finally caught up to him, Ron faded out of consciousness.

Justin was on his beach towel, unaware of the struggle. When he looked up and saw Mike in the chest-deep surf trying to keep Ron's head above water, he stood up.

"Justin! Justin! HELP!" Mike screamed as he saw Justin get up.

Justin ran to Mike and shouted, "What happened?"

"I don't know, I don't know. But you gotta help me!" Mike was frantic, babbling and completely exhausted.

Justin grabbed one of Ron's arms and Mike the other. They tried hauling him toward the beach but found that the motion of the waves kept dunking his head. They grabbed his hair to keep his head above the water while trying to run with him across the twenty yards of water. Conscious again, Ron remembers feeling the bones grinding in his neck as they struggled to move his nearly 200 pounds to dry land.

In just inches of water, Mike and Justin stopped. Mike couldn't go any further and told Justin to find help. The two brothers were alone, wet, covered in sand and exhausted. Ron didn't think he'd make it off of the beach alive.

"I'm gonna die, Mike," Ron gasped. His lungs weren't working right. "I love you, little brother. Tell Mom, Dad and Pennie that I love them, too." The words came out in a halting manner as his world faded.

"No, Ron!" Mike didn't know what was going to happen, but he knew what to do when all seems lost. He held Ron's face between his two trembling hands, Ron's back resting on his knees. Then he turned his face upward, swallowed a sob and closed his eyes.

"Oh, God," he shouted. "don't let my brother die! Please don't let Ronnie die!"

The young boy's prayers were answered.

Justin found a woman sunbathing just down the beach, briefly explained the situation and sent her to call 911. When the ambulance arrived, she was waiting in the parking lot to lead the emergency responders to Ron's location on the beach. They rushed him to the hospital.

Ron's neck had been broken in four places.

When Ron dove into the surf that day, he relied on one person and one person alone: himself. As he made his way into the water, Ron was thinking about how he was going to master surfing like he had mastered so many sports. He wasn't thinking about his faith, his family or his friends. As a seventeen-year-old football star with model good looks, Ron Heagy's life revolved around Ron Heagy. It was the Ronnie show, all the time. His parents were there to help him. His brother was there to hassle and worship him. Girlfriends provided a different kind of adoration. Sure, God was there, on Sundays. But like his parents, his spiritual life was more about rules than a relationship.

Ron Heagy almost died that spring day on the beach. By his own teenage standards, Ron's life ended that day. Everything he lived for was impossible from that day forward. As he eventually realized, his life began anew when he awoke paralyzed in the hospital. Up until his accident, Ron's focus had been on himself. His physical "disability" forced him to focus on what really matters in life.

Traction

Seventy percent of Ron's spinal cord was severed. Ron knew that if Mike hadn't pulled him from the water he would have drowned. Even in the hospital, however, Ron's survival wasn't guaranteed. Because the spinal cord was damaged so severely and so close to the brain, he only had partial control of his diaphragm, the muscle that allows the lungs to fill and collapse. He could breathe, but his breaths were shallow and he was constantly on the edge of unconsciousness.

Ron's parents arrived from Oregon overwhelmed with questions about their son's condition. Terry and Ron Sr. were concerned that his lack of total control of his diaphragm meant their son would be on life support. Ron's mom asked the doctor how long he would have to be on a respirator. The doctor hesitated a moment before answering, "Indefinitely."

Connected to all types of medical machines and monitoring systems, Ron held on to life with the hope that he would soon be better. He had plans. He had a football scholarship and dreams of playing in the pros. Living life in a wheelchair paralyzed from the neck down wasn't part of those plans. His family supported his hopeful attitude, even when the doctors seemed skeptical.

The next step in Ron's recovery was fusing the shattered vertebrae in his neck. The bones would be wired together to help give his head and neck some stability. When the surgery was finally green-lighted for the following day, Ron's courage lasted until just after midnight.

At 2:00 a.m. the phone rang in the house where Ron's parents were staying. Knowing that nothing good comes from a call that late at night, Ron's mom was glad to hear the nurse explain that her son wanted to talk to his parents.

"Talk? He's talking?" For the two weeks Ron had been on the respirator, his speech had trickled to a barely audible whisper. What his mom didn't know was that he'd persuaded the nurse to close off the opening from his tracheotomy and hold the phone to his lips.

"Mom?"

"Ronnie, are you all right?"

"I'm fine. I just—I just wanted to tell you and Dad that I love you."

After two weeks of silence, he was overcome with a need to speak to them, to tell them how much he appreciated the support and courage they gave him. His mom reassured him that they would be there during the surgery, that it was sure to go well and, most importantly, that God was with him.

The surgery took five hours. His parents were relieved to hear that the surgeons successfully scraped away the crushed bone and fused the broken vertebrae.

For Ron, however, the surgery didn't feel like the successes he had experienced in the past. Now, his days were long and full of seemingly endless cycles of treatments, pain and quiet boredom disrupted only by the thoughtful acts of visitors and staff members.

Ron started getting worried when, instead of the spectacular surge in his recovery that he'd hoped would happen, he started getting worse. He was too nauseous to eat so they fed him intravenously. He lost weight and started running a fever. He was sedated most of the time. Pressure sores which had developed on his heels became infected. The doctors tried taking him off his respirator but, when his breathing became too labored, they had to reconnect him to it.

Ron's doctors discovered a massive stress ulcer in his stomach which was causing the decline in Ron's health. The ulcer was cauterized with a saline solution as the doctors tried to reboot his digestive system. It didn't go well. The nasogastric tube that snaked through his nose and down into his stomach to feed him started causing sores in his nose and mouth. The drugs he was on to reduce his suffering caused hellacious dreams and hallucinations.

Now my misery is complete, Ron thought to himself. He wished he could tear out the tubes, pull out the respirator and breathe on his own. While he was wishing, he might as well wish that he could walk again. As bad as Ron felt physically, he felt even worse for his parents. As much as he and his mom needed his dad there, he had to go back to work at the paper mill in Oregon so they wouldn't lose their insurance.

Soon after Ron's dad left, Ron was visiting with a guest when his eyes rolled back into his head and he passed out. The ICU staff began CPR immediately.

Ron's heart stopped once during the surgery to save him. While he was unconscious, he dreamed that he could hear his deceased grandfather talking in the distance. For the first time since his accident, Ron was experiencing no pain. It felt like heaven.

When Ron woke up, he realized he was in the hospital and that his dad was standing beside his bed reading from the Bible.

"Consider it pure joy, my brothers, whenever you face trials of many kinds," his father read.

Joy? Was he kidding? Ron couldn't feel below his neck. Each day brought more suffering. Ron knew that he wasn't feeling pure joy.

Despite Ron's doubts about God's role in his life at that point, the Heagys' prayers kept getting answered.

Part of the difficulty with Ron's care was how far away he was from friends and family. His parents had been by his side since they'd heard about his accident, but his dad couldn't exactly commute to work from L.A. Even though Ron Sr. believed that his place was with his wife and son, he needed his job and accompanying health insurance to help pay the medical bills. The price of transportation to get Ron to Good Samaritan Hospital in Portland was going to take yet another loan. Before they added to their skyrocketing medical debt, Ron's parents heard about another patient from Portland who needed transportation to L.A. The two families agreed to split the price of the charter flight.

The day before leaving for Portland, Ron's mom washed his hair and shaved his face. He smiled, thinking about his old routine of two showers a day. He hadn't had a shower in five weeks.

"You look downright handsome," his mom said as she combed his hair. "Here, see for yourself."

When she held the mirror in front of his face, the skinny guy who stared back looked only slightly familiar. Ron had lost more that fifty pounds. His skin was pasty white, his cheeks were hollow and his eyes had a sad dullness that remained even when he smiled. That's when the reality caught up to Ron. He would never look the way he had before his injury. His future was gone, crushed like the vertebrae in his neck. He began to wonder: What was the point of it all?

At Good Samaritan Hospital, Ron was transferred to a circular frame bed, but he didn't think of the change as an upgrade. In a Stryker bed in L.A., he was moved from lying face up to lying face down by a sideways rotation similar to a log rolling in water. The circular frame bed rotated around like a Ferris wheel, and it wasn't made for patients any taller than six feet. He'd spent weeks lying horizontal. As the new bed rotated, it elevated Ron's upper body, working his heart more than he was accustomed to. Without enough blood getting to Ron's head, he would black out every time they rotated him.

Ron's new bed wasn't too thrilled with him, either. At six feet two inches, Ron saw that his feet protruded past the end of the frame. As the bed revolved, his feet would drag along the floor, causing the motor to overheat. Ron sensed some overheating of the medical staff's patience, too. With each rotation Ron passed in and out of consciousness which caused a pounding headache. Each rotation also brought the bed closer to a complete mechanical failure. Ron's feelings of frustration and worthlessness were gaining ground.

Terry stayed with him during the weekdays and Ron Sr. came to Portland on the weekends to give her a break. Ron could tell that his dad was trying to hide his worries about the mounting medical expenses. Even though Ron didn't see the bills, he sensed the tension. *Someday, after I'm well and playing professional football, I'll make it up to them!*

Ron couldn't make his bed any bigger or his body any smaller, but one of the constant aggravations that he could try to do something about was the respirator. Once he could breathe without the respirator, he could start rehabilitation. Yet breathing without the respirator seemed impossible. When the technician cut his assisted breath rate to three per minute, Ron nearly suffocated. Each breath required a conscious effort. He fought to pull air into his lungs then push it out. He was afraid to fall asleep, scared that he wouldn't awaken because he forgot to breathe during the night. Between his exertion and stress, his temperature climbed to 103 degrees. The pulmonary specialist tried talking the family into accepting the fact that Ron would have to use a respirator for the rest of his life. Trying to soften the blow, the specialist explained that portable respirators could be installed in wheelchairs. It wasn't what Ron wanted to hear.

After signing a waiver, the Heagys were allowed to try weaning Ron from the breathing machine. Terry's strategy was to remove the respirator during the day to increase his breathing ability and then reattach it at night.

Ron recovered one breath at a time. After two months of breathless muttering, the respirator was wheeled away and Ron's voice was free. It was the beginning of a rejuvenation. He could talk to his sister Pennie and his brother Mike. He could share his struggles with his parents and get their support in return. He could communicate directly with therapists, doctors and specialists.

Ron's victory over the ventilator gave him hope. He felt that it signified an almost divine blessing that meant he would win the battle against his paralysis. The experts had said breathing without a ventilator was impossible, yet Ron was breathing on his own. If he could prove the experts wrong once, what could stop him from proving them wrong twice? Free of the ventilator, he began physical therapy.

On Memorial Day, Ron moved down the hall to a shared room. His new roommate was Jimmy, an eight-year-old who had been hit by a car while riding his bike. He'd been in a coma since his accident. The other big change was that Terry headed back to Brownsville. Ron wasn't thrilled about either change, but Jimmy didn't say much and Ron understood that his mom was going to prepare the house for his eventual release from the hospital.

Ron put on a brave face and told his mom that he'd be fine.

He began therapy with the mindset that he would soon be kissing his wheelchair goodbye. When other quadriplegics told him how rewarding life can be even in a chair, Ron listened politely but didn't understand what they were trying to say. One patient told Ron that he'd been paralyzed for eleven years. *Eleven years? I would rather die than be in a wheelchair that long.*

He just knew he was going to get better.

The day that Ron finally mastered steering his power chair with his chin was a glorious one. Ron felt as free as anyone with two working legs. He could go anywhere, do anything.

After a few days of enjoying his new freedom, Ron finally understood what the chair really meant. The insurance company handing over a $9,000 check for the chair could only mean that it didn't think he was getting better. Ron realized that some of the patients who had started rehab at the same time he had were already using walkers or crutches. Taking stock of his own progress, Ron couldn't feel much improvement in his disconnected nerves.

He finally brought up his apparent lack of progress to one of the physical therapists. Not wanting to give Ron the wrong information, the therapist recommended that Ron talk to his doctor.

A few days after the dead-end conversation, Ron and his parents met with his doctors. Even though the meeting was about Ron, the doctors spoke directly to his parents.

"Mr. and Mrs. Heagy, we have tried to help your son regain at least partial mobility. At first we thought feeling might return to his arms, but it hasn't." The doctor paused. "I think our consensus now is that there is nothing more we can do for him. We've tried everything."

"Maybe *you* have given up, doctor, but we haven't," Ron Sr. said.

"There has to be something we haven't tried yet," Terry insisted.

"Mrs. Heagy, please believe me. I know how you feel," the doctor continued. "But your son's injuries are permanent. Too many nerves were severed during the accident. They can't be regained. If Ron were my son, I would take him home and help him adjust." He paused again. "Or you might consider a full-care facility."

Ron's dad stood to his feet. "That isn't an option, sir. Our son won't be put in a home for the disabled as long as I am alive."

Too stunned to speak, Ron sat quietly in his wheelchair as the medical staff solemnly filed out of the room. His mom and dad were also quiet but, as his mom reached across and took Ron's hand, she whispered, "We're not giving up, Ronnie."

His parents tucked Ron in that night, getting his sheets tight around his sides and up to his chin, just like they had done when he was a little boy. No matter what happens, they said, God had a plan for him and he shouldn't worry. That's not what Ron thought. Then, as a family, they prayed for Ron to have a good night's rest and they said their goodbyes. Ron managed to hold back his tears until he could no longer hear their footsteps in the hall. Then the dam broke.

Once the sobbing started, he couldn't control it. He wanted the pain to stop and the disappointment to end. He wanted it all to be over. What else could he do? He was a burden on everyone he knew. The doctors couldn't fix him. His parents were going to have to take care of him for the rest of his life. He would never again be able to hold a girl's hand.

That night, as he cried, he begged God to end his life. If he couldn't be a man, there wasn't any point to living.

In the darkness Ron heard a small voice.

"Ronnnn."

He held his breath, listening. Had someone come into his room? How embarrassing would that be? He tried bringing his sobs down to gasps.

"Ronnnn."

It was Jimmy, who hadn't said a word the entire time he'd laid in the bed next to Ron's. He was in a coma, right? Ron stopped crying as he tried to figure out what was going on.

Ron felt slightly guilty because he had ignored the boy since they had become hospital roommates. In a way, he had considered his comatose roommate an inconvenience. As bad as Ron felt for himself, Jimmy's situation was even worse. And now the kid was reaching across the sea of hopelessness, tossing a lifeline to the sobbing man in the other bed.

"Ron," the little voice whispered again. "I—I love you."

That night was the first and last time Ron heard Jimmy's voice. Ron doesn't doubt that he heard the little boy; if he hadn't, Ron would have cried all night. Jimmy reminded Ron that, as bad as Ron's situation was for him, it could be worse. Ron could be on death's door, kept alive by machines. What if Mike hadn't been there to save him? Even just a little longer in the water or slightly more damage to his spinal cord would have made Ron's prognosis much more dire.

The words Ron heard that night changed his perspective and made him realize that he is never truly alone.

Ron attacked therapy with a new drive. Maybe he wasn't going to be a famous pro football star. Maybe he couldn't hold a girlfriend's hand, but he had a sharp mind and great communication skills. Ron could reach out to others who were hurting the way that Jimmy had reached out to him. Ron was going to succeed in ways he might not be able to imagine. He simply had to believe.

Home

Life got even better when the hospital finally released Ron. Leaving the community of experts and support staff was a little scary for him, but Ron's family believed that they could handle all of his needs at home. Though he was leaving the support of the hospital, he was returning to the tight, loving embrace of his family. After so many years of taking them for granted, Ron was just starting to realize the power of their love for him.

The Heagys were a close-knit family before Ron's injury; their bonds became even stronger. Working as a team, they took care of Ron's waking and sleeping needs. A common problem for almost all people with paralysis is the development of pressure sores from lying in the same position for long lengths of time, so someone was on duty at night to awaken and change Ron's sleeping position.

Ron worried that the constant care he required was becoming a tremendous burden on his family, especially when family members were forgetful or expressed any sign of frustration or impatience. He felt his positive attitude slipping. Dark thoughts were becoming darker as he found more and more evidence that he was wasting everyone's time. He felt worthless and helpless at the same time. Maybe he hadn't really heard Jimmy's voice in the hospital—maybe it had all been a trick of his mind. He couldn't think of a worse way to live, constantly being such a worrisome responsibility on everyone who loved him. The pressure wasn't fair to his family.

Ron had hit rock-bottom. He began thinking about a way he could permanently exit from life.

Trying to find a quadriplegic-friendly method of suicide was, in itself, an exercise in willpower and critical thinking. Ron spent his free time running through the list of possibilities. He could roll off a cliff, but he needed help getting to the cliff. He couldn't tie a noose in a rope nor could he hold a razor blade. He thought about drowning, which had distinct possibilities. Though he had regained the ability to breathe on his own, he still couldn't cough well.

Committed to end his life, Ron seized the opportunity when his dad rolled him into the shower one Saturday. After his dad left, Ron tilted his head back, deeply inhaling the warm water into his lungs. His lack of diaphragmatic power made the natural reactions of gagging and coughing futile. When his dad returned a few minutes later, he found Ron gasping for air underneath the shower stream. He raised Ron's arms and slapped him on the back, asking him what had happened.

At first he wasn't going to explain but, after his dad continued with direct, pointed questions, Ron's resolve broke and he told his dad everything. Thankfully his dad was there for him.

Medical and therapy staff members in the hospital had made sure that Ron was prepared for the physical hardships that awaited him when he left. He learned to write with his head and mouth as well as steer his chair with his chin. He understood about blood pressure fluctuations, bed sores and dealing with a bladder that no longer responded to nerve stimulation. Yet Ron had never received the mental and emotional tools to help him live life as a quadriplegic. It wasn't that the experts hadn't tried helping him understand what his life was going to be like; however, much of what they tried teaching him assumed that he had already reached a certain level of mental development.

Paralysis doesn't come with a manual. Neither does adulthood. Ron hadn't turned 18 when he dove into the Huntington Beach surf. It wasn't that he was immature—he just still had a lot of mental growing to do. He was a sharp, good-looking and athletic kid. With little effort, everything he had tried to do he wound up doing well. He had won over girls as easily as he had won football games for the team.

Almost dying in the ocean was the first major setback of Ron's short life. As "character building" experiences go, paralysis is a doozy. Facing such a devastating setback at such a young age, Ron had very little life experience to fall back on. He needed to develop abilities to deal with the physical effects of paralysis as well as develop the essential mental and emotional abilities to survive life as a quadriplegic.

He began to get the hang of the situation he found himself in. His family had never wavered in their support and, as

Ron realized how taking his own life would be selfish, suicide was no longer an option. The only option left was life. How could he live his life when it took so much work to simply get into his chair every morning? He decided to talk to his grandma, who had raised his dad along with eight other aunts and uncles on virtually no money and with tremendous grace. He asked her how she did it.

"I did it one day at a time, Ronnie. One day at a time." She knew that he wasn't asking about raising nine kids, so she added, "And that's what you've got to do now. Don't look back. Don't worry about tomorrow. Just take it one day at a time."

Keeping her counsel in mind, Ron didn't get so depressed when things weren't going well. Quite a few days, Ron needed to practice his grandma's advice.

Drawing from the everyday inspiration of his family, Ron found paths to victory. Instead of dwelling on the necessity of having more surgery, multiple bladder infections and incontinence problems, Ron looked for something positive to do. After finding fellow quadriplegic Joni Eareckson Tada's inspirational books about painting without using her arms, Ron enrolled in a local community college's beginning art class. Ron describes his first attempts at drawing with a charcoal pencil clenched in his mouth as pathetic. But he didn't give up. By the end of the semester he could use a pen or pencil with some skill, and he finished with a C in the class, along with some encouraging words from the instructor.

When he visited his sister's summer camp with his mom and dad, a camp staffer asked him to speak to the other teenagers about his struggles and victories. As a football star, he had loved the attention of the crowd during a winning game, which filled him with pride. In his wheelchair, he felt that people were staring at him out of pity; he worried that his self-esteem would spiral downward if he tried to talk only to stumble over his words. He didn't want to do it but, seeing the excited reactions of his mom and dad, Ron decided to speak to the group.

To his surprise, he discovered that telling his story came naturally even without any notes or preparation. He received warm applause at the speech's conclusion and, even better, some of the teenagers came up afterward to talk to him. For the first time since his injury, Ron felt that he had found his calling. It wasn't football and it wasn't wrestling—it was something Ron could do whether or not he was in a wheelchair. This was what he had been waiting for, and it was better than a cure.

In his teenage sister's summer camp, Ron had caught a glimpse of his future.

As part of his positive push forward, Ron enrolled at Linn-Benton Community College. Despite studying hard, he was still surprised to find an A at the top of his first algebra test. It was in his algebra class that he met Julie, an attractive coed with a brother who used a wheelchair. She introduced herself to Ron during class one day and, by the time it was over, they were friends. After spending time together studying, they eventually started seeing each other socially. Soon they were going steady.

With Julie by his side, Ron took the leap into independent living. Though his worried parents expressed some concern, Ron argued that they couldn't take care of him forever. The sooner he learned how to manage his own budget and live with the assistance of a caregiver, the better. With his Social Security allowance, Ron rented a low-income apartment in nearby Lebanon, Oregon.

Julie stayed by Ron's side through a prolonged battle with kidney stones which eventually required two surgeries. Since Julie had already proven that she would stand by him through sickness and poor times—times couldn't get much worse, could they?—Ron decided that he had better ask her to marry him so she'd be around for the healthier, richer times. They were married in April 1984. While Julie was planning their perfect wedding, Ron was planning their perfect future.

Their future started right after the honeymoon. Ron transferred to Christian Heritage College near San Diego where he studied psychology. Julie became his caregiver and study partner. When he wasn't studying, he found a job many would say was ill-suited for a quadriplegic: He flipped old cars. First, he would find a worthwhile restoration project. By hiring a willing yet inexperienced laborer, he could simultaneously provide valuable experience to the worker and rebuild the car to a marketable condition.

It wasn't an easy life, especially for Julie, but the newlyweds made it through the four years together. After graduation, Ron found a job in Lebanon at East Linn Christian

Academy, where he taught classes on the Bible, English and, yes, automotive maintenance. Ron believed that he finally had a chance at a normal life. He worked as hard as he had ever worked to become the perfect teacher. It wasn't enough to ensure that each one of his students had an opportunity for one-on-one instruction; Ron also made himself available during breaks and after school in case a student needed someone to talk to.

While Ron was becoming a favorite of students and parents, Julie stayed at home. Her friends had been studying for college degrees while she was helping Ron secure his degree. Even after his graduation, her life was devoted to providing the care Ron needed to have the life that he wanted—that he thought they both wanted.

The role of caregiver became too suffocating for Julie. She finally told Ron about her frustrations: She had not completed her own education and she had no career. Ron realized that the entire time that Julie had been taking care of him he hadn't been taking care of her. He had inverted his priorities, putting his needs over hers. Ron immediately promised to change, but the commitment came too late. The next day, Ron came home from work to discover an empty house and a note.

At his loneliest point ever, Ron became more introspective. He soon understood that his pride had pushed Julie away. He had thought that he was doing everything for the marriage, for their future together, but Ron realized that his actions had been for his own benefit. He had believed that he was accomplishing his goals all by himself; it wasn't until Julie left that Ron understood how much she'd helped him achieve so much of what he had sought. Focused on proving that a guy in a wheelchair could be successful, he had lost sight of Julie's needs. Now, without Julie, all the things that had meant so much to Ron no longer seemed very important.

Master's Degree

Ron first met Daniel Webster Doe after he responded to a Social Services ad for a live-in caregiver. Doe was a big, burly man sporting a leopard tattoo on his arm and a long, bushy beard. To Ron he looked more like a bar bouncer than a caregiver. Contrary to his appearance, Daniel Doe was a kind, competent caregiver whose personality was a perfect yang to Ron's yin.

Though they were technically still married, Ron didn't have any contact with Julie after she left him. He sent her letters, but they came back unopened. No one from her family would tell him where she was. Feeling like he needed a fresh start, Ron applied to San Diego State University graduate school. The one problem was that Daniel Doe only agreed to go to California with Ron temporarily—he didn't want to live there.

Ron's academic career at San Diego State wasn't as smooth as it had been for his undergraduate degree. His days were full of classes, studying and the ongoing struggle to find a dependable caregiver. Wally was the first failure. After their first weekend together, Wally stole Ron's ATM card and withdrew

$400 while Ron was in class on Monday. A string of duds and disappointments followed.

His classes weren't going very well, either. While pursuing a master's degree in social work, Ron was surprised to be met with indifference and scorn from some professors. Whenever he was asked by doubters how he expected to earn a master's degree in his "condition," Ron recalled one special woman's words of wisdom.

"One day at a time," Ron would calmly tell each one. "I'm just going to take it one day at a time."

The first year of graduate school didn't get any easier for Ron when Julie showed up on his doorstep. When she stayed for a visit, Ron thought that he finally had a chance to patch up their relationship.

Julie left after a week. It would be their last goodbye. The divorce papers arrived a few weeks later.

When summer break finally came, Ron went back to his family's home in Brownsville to relax and recharge his batteries. During the summer, he briefly reconnected with Ann, one of his old students. As a teacher, he had helped her deal with a family member's death. When Ron had free time during his busy summer, he and Ann would get together. They were just two friends, talking about their lives and sharing their problems. At first there was nothing particularly special about their time together, but soon Ron could feel a romantic connection developing. As excited as he felt, he was scared about committing to another relationship so soon after the last one ended.

Toward the end of the summer, Ron began screening potential caregivers who would be willing to drive him down to San Diego. He settled on an older applicant who boasted a PhD and teaching experience. Once again, Ron thought he had a winner. He said goodbye to Ann and the two friends promised that they would stay in touch.

The drive to San Diego was a disaster. During each pit stop, Ron's caregiver would take a brief walk to stretch her legs. Ron didn't realize that she was drinking alcohol as she walked around. Imagine this scene: a van pulled over to the side of the road with a female driver passed out and slumped over the steering wheel as a quadriplegic tries to fix a flat tire by himself. When the pair finally made it to San Diego at 2:30 a.m., the woman collapsed into bed, where she stayed for three days.

Within a two-week period, the caregiver was sober, recovering and then back to passed-out drunk. Ron had to resort to more expensive yet dependable agency-provided caregivers.

Despite the rocky start, Ron's second year at San Diego State was a great one. He met Dave Woods, who became an all-star friend and co-conspirator in many of Ron's schemes, which included finding ways of staying in touch with Ann.

Time away from Ann gave Ron room to think about the next step in their relationship. He decided that he wouldn't let the opportunity pass him by. After spring midterms he asked

Ann—the funny, smart and pretty woman whom he loved and who loved him in return—to marry him. She said yes.

Back from his mission to Oregon to ask Ann to be his wife, Ron received a call from his old friend Daniel. After talking to Ron, Daniel agreed to come down to San Diego as Ron's caregiver. Finally, Ron didn't have to worry about whether there was food in the fridge or money missing from his bank account.

During an internship as a counselor at a local school, Ron rediscovered how well his disability allowed him to connect with kids. This time, the kids he connected with thought that their futures were so hopeless, so bleak, that they had no reason to live. It was the most rewarding work Ron had done, and he felt that he had finally found his true purpose in life. During one intense session with a suicidal boy, Ron gestured to a painting on the wall of his office.

"Do you know how I painted that picture?"

The boy shrugged.

"I held a paintbrush in my mouth."

"It must be a paint-by-number picture," he said after standing up to take a closer look.

"Nope," Ron said, laughing. "It's an original."

"That's hard to believe, man."

"I want you to have it," Ron replied. "Take that painting off the wall and hang it in your room. Whenever you're feeling down, look at that painting and remember what we've talked about today. Think of all the things you have to be thankful for and all the things you can accomplish if you try."

He had no doubt now that counseling was what he was supposed to do. But determining his career path was only part of the answer to finding happiness.

With graduation behind him, Ron moved back to Oregon. He and Ann were married in July in a simple ceremony in Albany, Oregon.

While he tried to line up a career as a school counselor, Ron took on what he thought was a one-time speaking engagement at a local high school. That's when he reconnected with the joyful experience he had while speaking at his sister's summer camp. He believed that he had found a completely new calling: motivational speaker. Ron pursued his new passion the same way he had attacked his teaching career—with single-minded vigor. Sometimes this meant driving across states, like a rock band on tour, to speak at schools and churches. Unlike a rock band, no roadies or advance staff helped to carry the load. It was just Ron and Ann, and the tours barely made enough for them to cover expenses.

Ron was inspired, however, and it wasn't just his speaking opportunities that inspired him. After he discovered a thirty-four-acre ranch for sale near Albany, he decided it was a perfect spot for a wheelchair-accessible summer camp he wanted to name Camp Attitude. Ron and Ann struggled to get the land purchased and the camp built and permitted. Finally, in

August 2000, the camp opened its doors to 1,000 supporters from six different states.

By 2002 the pair had been together through so much: the early days of Ron's speaking career; trying and failing to get pregnant; the eventual adoption of their baby girl, Roni; the construction of Ron's camp. Ann and Ron's marriage buckled under the stress. His second marriage had lasted longer than his first, but it followed a similar trajectory. Ron pursued the girl, won the girl and, with the help of the girl, went after his professional goals. After their marriage's amicable end, Ron came to the conclusion that surviving life was his specialty. His personal example of perseverance was an inspiration to thousands. Yet he wanted to know why he kept failing in his personal relationships.

Although Ron was a nice guy with a great attitude about life, he knew that he still held on to the old male priorities of looks and professional success. He saw women as thoughtful, spiritual people but he realized that he might have ignored some of Ann's needs in order to pursue his own interests. He had determined that the same issues had undermined his marriage with Julie.

Thankfully, Ron knew plenty about changing one's attitudes, including his own. It might be too late for Ann and him to save their marriage—there was too much history there. Could he make it work with another woman? Would he ever be able to create a loving, sustainable partnership?

Harmony

Even in his wheelchair, Ron was good at being the hero. Everything about how Ron had met and courted his first two wives could have originated in a storybook romance. However, nothing with Kelli went according to his plan, not even the romantic elements. Kelli was hired by Ann as a part-time bookkeeper as Ron and Ann tried to sort out their marriage. At first, Ron felt threatened by the new employee who was hired by his wife to keep him accountable, but they soon became friends. Their proximity meant that they talked and shared personal experiences and opinions, and it was largely Kelli's influence that helped Ron see how his traditional male pride tainted many of his personal relationships. What started as a platonic relationship developed into emotional feelings, and Ron and Kelli realized that they couldn't have any more contact with one another.

Meanwhile, Ron and Ann sought counseling to save their marriage but without success. During the same period, Kelli also tried to patch up her own marriage but ended up getting divorced. A year passed. Ron knew he was depressed but he had no one to talk to. His parents had moved out of the state; raw nerves about the way Ron had responded to his sister's divorce had created friction within his family. Suffering, he isolated himself.

Despite being a gifted counselor and an inspirational speaker, Ron was unable to fix what was broken. After all that had happened, having a relationship with Kelli seemed wrong.

Not being with her, not being able to talk to her about his fears and dreams, also seemed wrong. Ron's second divorce reinforced his sense of failure, but losing contact with Kelli felt like he had become paralyzed all over again.

When he finally contacted Kelli, it was like the atrophied nerves began firing again. They started dating and, even though it had been a year since his divorce, Ron's pursuit of Kelli struck some of his friends as inappropriate. Ron didn't want to upset his friends but, together again with his best friend, he felt that his life finally was balanced. He was happy. When Kelli and Ron married in October 2003, Kelli brought two girls from her previous marriage to live with Ron and Roni in Albany.

About six months after their wedding, Kelli walked by with her head down as Ron rolled into his office. She was crying.

"What's wrong?" Ron asked.

"It's nothing. Don't worry," Kelli replied. "I can't talk about it right now. We will talk about it later when everyone has gone and you have no other distractions."

Ron could tell that something was wrong and, after two failed marriages, he wasn't looking forward to finding out what latent issue there might be. He trusted Kelli more than anyone else, so he put his anxiety aside.

When he got back from his meetings that day, Kelli met him with a smile. "Ron, I'm sorry for being upset earlier," she said.

Before Ron could ask what had upset her that morning, he noticed a vase of flowers on the desk. That puzzled him. He didn't usually get flowers when Kelli was upset. He wheeled around to check them out. Concealed in the arrangement was an odd stick. It looked like a thermometer.

"What is this?"

Kelli opened the card so he could read it. Its meaning finally dawned on him.

"Are you pregnant?"

She smiled. "Yes, that's why I was crying this morning."

"Uh—how did you do that?"

"What do you mean? *You* did it," she fired back with a smirk. Did she have to draw him a picture?

"It's not possible.... The doctors said.... It's been twenty-four years. I've been in my chair, and—and I'm old."

"I think the facts speak for themselves."

"We've done nothing, well, besides, you know. This means that you have conceived naturally." Ron still couldn't believe it.

When Ron was able to hear the heartbeat of his baby racing 167 beats per minute on the ultrasound, he accepted the fact: They were going to have a little miracle.

Gracie Lee was born in January 2005.

Basking in the beautiful blessing that his family had received, Ron thought about the dark times in his life and finally understood. When he focused on the good things—his faith, family and friends—life was sweet and success came easily. When he tried to heroically achieve what he wanted and ignored the needs and advice of his friends, he soon found himself alone, miserable and in dire straits. Ron realized that sometimes his need to prove what he can accomplish—despite his broken body—was greater than his willingness to accept life's lessons. He finally understood that it wasn't his wheelchair that kept getting in the way of having a successful, rewarding life. It was his pride.

It took years for Ron to learn to let go of the guilt he experienced; he didn't feel that he deserved all of the attention, the energy and effort necessary to keep him alive and thriving. Now he realizes that everyone has trials; in Ron's case, however, his larger, physical challenges are visible to others. When learning of his numerous accomplishments, it's easy to forget that this man who is living a so-called "normal" life—full of disappointments as well as moments of great joy—is trapped in a body that doesn't move.

Ron admits that there have been moments when he has felt like giving up, but he doesn't allow his mind to stay in that place because he believes that being crippled is only a state of mind. Instead, he focuses on his purpose and potential. He knows that others need him.

Ron developed "The Never Give Up Creed" to help others succeed. He suggests signing it and placing it somewhere that you will read it every day.

The Creed

I believe my life has purpose and value.

I will pursue my purpose daily.

I will set my goals and not allow the negativity of others to distract me in achieving them.

I am the master of my attitude.

Today I choose to be positive.

I will love life and press on in the midst of my struggles.

I believe I can, therefore, I will.

I will tap my full potential and with the help of others we will reach dreams that on our own are not possible.

I will be strong to the finish and I will never give up.

In the end when I lay my head down, I will rest in peace, because I have faith, hope and love.

Ron closes the creed by adding, "I believe in You…You are loved."

Anyone who has had the great pleasure of meeting him or being in one of his audiences knows that Ron Heagy is an inspiring individual who walks the walk he speaks about—by rolling on.

*Source Material**

Heagy, Ron and Dryer, Donita. *Life is an Attitude.* (Second Edition) 2005.

Heagy, Ron. Roll on Ron/Never Give Up. www.rollonron.com.

———. Speaking Information. www.ronheagy.com.

*Used with permission from Ron Heagy

It's Not What Happens To You, It's What You Do About It

The W Mitchell Story

W Mitchell is more than the name of an incredible man. The simple story of how the man who calls himself Mitchell got his name is a perfect example of how someone can choose his own path in life, right down to the name the world knows him by.

As a young man and recent arrival to San Francisco, Mitchell found out that a name change in California was as simple as changing the name on your driver's license. He chose the letter W as a passing reference to his birth name, William John Schiff III, and Mitchell to honor his stepfather who had passed away while Mitchell was in his teens. This was the 1960s, and rebellion was in the air, which suited Mitchell just fine. His mom once observed that where a "Do Not Enter" sign was posted, Mitchell saw an open invitation.

After flunking out of sixth grade, his concerned parents sent Mitchell to a psychologist who determined that he was a "gifted underachiever." After flunking seventh grade, he found himself in military school, where his parents hoped he would find the structure he needed. Fourteen-year-old Mitchell loved it at the Augusta Military Academy. He didn't particularly care for the rules, though. "Lights out" meant that the staff literally cut the power to the dorm rooms. Mitchell drilled a hole in the wall, ran power from the bathroom into his room, plugged in the radio and the lights, and hung blankets over the windows so he and his friends wouldn't get caught. Young Mitchell did well at the academy, despite his proclivity for trouble. Seeing his success as a sign of reform, his parents transferred him to a boarding school, where he was in constant hot water. He eventually found himself back in public school.

After the death of his stepfather in 1960, Mitchell was sick of bouncing from school to school. The Marines wouldn't let a seventeen-year-old join up, so Mitchell went to his dad who signed the form permitting him to enlist.

Life was sometimes confusing in the Corps. Mitchell scored in the top 20 percent on the aptitude test. The Corps rewarded him with the job of loading ordinance onto warplanes. A weapons instructor noticed Mitchell reading a book while waiting for flamethrower instruction. In a personal version of *Fahrenheit 451*, during class Mitchell obliterated his copy of *Hawaii* with a fiery stream.

Once he was out of the service, Mitchell found himself watching the sun set on the golden age of the hippie in San Francisco.

Motorcycles. Flight lessons. Working as a cable car gripman. Mitchell's life developed along the theme of gears and speed in San Francisco. Dating back to the 1870s, the San Francisco cable car is a simple yet tricky vehicle to move through the city. Cables constantly running under the tracks at ten miles an hour are grabbed by a manual lever in the cable car.

A gripman must be strong enough to operate the grip, smart enough to know when to coast, and daring enough to take on the bicycle, pedestrian and vehicle traffic of the city. To this day, only about 30% of the trainees graduate from training. It was the perfect job for Mitchell.

Always a restless soul, Mitchell felt himself settling down. The double shifts he worked on the cable cars—sixteen hour days that he loved every minute of—gave him some money to play with. Time off meant more flight lessons, skiing in Colorado, or motoring around the city on a motorcycle. His life wasn't perfect, but it was pretty darn close.

In fact, Mitchell describes the morning of July 19, 1971, as perfection. That morning he'd taken his first solo flight, an experience he describes simply as "orgasmic." He was riding up South Van Ness on a two-day-old Honda 750, the meanest, fastest, biggest bike on the street.

That's when hell opened its maw and tried swallowing Mitchell whole.

Phoenix Burns

The fireball was about ten feet high and four feet wide. A blue, intense heat burned with the ferocity of lit gasoline hitting oxygen. A crowd growing fifty feet away on the corner of 26th and South Van Ness could feel the fire's heat.

Mitchell didn't see the crowd. He saw the fireball—from inside of it.

Riding his Honda north along Van Ness that afternoon,

Mitchell had been thinking about his experiences that day and the wonderful life he was living. He felt like the King of San Francisco. To the left of Mitchell, a maroon laundry truck tooled along on the inside lane.

As they approached 26th, without warning the laundry truck hooked right, across Mitchell's lane of traffic. He hit the truck squarely in its side. The lid on Mitchell's gas tank popped open as he laid the bike on its side. With a loud WHOOSH, a fireball visible for several blocks erupted.

His life probably would have ended then and there if it hadn't been for a car salesman working nearby who grabbed a fire extinguisher and put Mitchell out. The ambulance arrived minutes later and raced him to San Francisco General Hospital.

In 1971, if a person suffered burns over seventy-five percent of his body, he was dead. With over 65 per cent of Mitchell's body burned, the doctors were not sure he would survive; they put his chances at fifty-fifty. Mitchell's helmet saved his scalp. His leather jacket saved most of his torso and arms. But much of the skin on his face and hands didn't survive the fire.

The human brain can only take so much trauma. As the emergency room staff cut off his still-smoldering clothes, Mitchell slipped into a deep coma where, with the aid of drugs, he would stay for weeks.

The coma was a blessing. The doctors had sewn his eyelids shut to keep his eyes moist. He had a tracheotomy tube inserted into his throat to help him breathe. He shrunk from 175 to 125 pounds. Visitors, including tough guys who had worked on the cable cars with Mitchell, sometimes fainted when seeing him for the first time.

The well-wishing from his visitors is one of the things that Mitchell remembers from that initial period of drug-addled semiconsciousness. When he finally surfaced, Mitchell wondered if consciousness was all that great. His eyes were still sewn shut and he was in an extraordinary amount of pain. Dr. Mark Gorney, the surgeon who worked on repairing Mitchell's damaged skin, put it like this: "Being extensively burned is the most catastrophic, painful, unimaginably difficult situation a human being can find himself in. In terms of pain, it is like being flayed alive every day."

Once his eyelids were able to open, the staff kept him away from mirrors and other reflective surfaces. In the back of his mind, Mitchell knew he would have to see himself—his new self—but recovery depends so much on positive attitude and strong willpower. He knew that if he took on too many challenges at once, he might upset his psyche's delicate balancing act.

Recovery began with healing the skin he still had. Mitchell's nerves screamed as the gurney took the frequent trip to the whirlpool for therapy. A burn victim will die from fluid loss or infection if left alone, so burn victims are never really left alone. Something excruciating is being done to them virtually every hour of the day, day after day. Skin is gently gurged away, grafted back on, stretched, squeezed, lubricated, bandaged and poked.

Mitchell had sixteen skin-graft surgeries in four months.

He couldn't see much. The contacts he'd worn the day of the accident had damaged the surface of his eyes. What he could see was always the same. The same fuzzy ceiling. The same hallway. The same whirlpool room. The medical staff in the burn ward was always the same and they were always inflicting pain.

Mitchell's life <u>was</u> the burn ward. His mind drew its own conclusion: He was in hell.

He shared this conclusion with his nurse. With the angelic sensibility of the special breed of people who make up burn unit nurses, Mitchell's nurse worked on changing Mitchell's perception.

She took him outside, let him smell and listen to the city. Mitchell's friends visited and brought his Great Dane named Puppy.

Puppy broke into a frenzy when he heard Mitchell's voice. He started scurrying around, trying to find the source of his master's voice. It had been so long! Where was he? It was a difficult riddle for a dog to solve Mitchell appeared different, smelled different. The voice was the only thing Puppy recognized.

The fast thinking of Mitchell's nurse pulled him back from the edge of severe depression. It was a turning point in his recovery.

When the doctors realized Mitchell was going to pull through, they decided something needed to be done about his hands. Another operation. More bandages. Mitchell started telling everyone who would listen that the surgery must have worked. He could feel his fingers moving in the bandages. He could even feel the texture of the bandages.

When the day came for the unveiling of his new hands, there was obvious tension in the room. Comments were made about how the surgeons needed to remove more tissue than planned, and that phantom limbs could make a person feel as if something that is actually gone is still there. The bandages unraveled and unraveled. Even after Mitchell's cloth-covered hands were fist-sized, the bandages continued to unravel.

Mitchell had no fingers. Small stumps were all that were left. The room fell silent.

"Wow," he finally said. "This is going to destroy my pool game."

Mitchell could have responded in an almost infinite number of ways. A justifiable reaction would have been moaning, wailing, cursing God, getting depressed, even the eventual taking of his own life. But he didn't bother with any of that.

Instead, Mitchell thought about his training in the Marines and the support of his family and friends. Once he had fingers, then he didn't. What this change meant was completely up to Mitchell. He could see it as the end of his life, a universal curse, or a challenge.

Mitchell decided it was a challenge.

The secret to Mitchell's mental survival was consciously

not realizing how terrible things were. To this day, he is proud to say that he still refuses to "know" how terrible it was. It's a simple way of saying that he refused to accept the social definition of what being horribly burned should mean. It's a subtle shift in expectations. Instead of focusing on what he should have looked like or the handsome lady-killer he used to look like, he focused on what he could do looking the way he did. When he viewed his life with a new perspective, he realized that not looking like he used to look didn't mean that he couldn't accomplish what he'd always wanted to accomplish.

As a cable car gripman, Mitchell was experienced in taking charge of a large, heavy vehicle full of oblivious commuters and getting them to their destination quickly and safely. He was used to responsibility. He was used to control. He looked different but, when he finally found his mental equilibrium, he was ready to get back to his old, take-charge self.

He put the nix on a move to a state-of-the-art burn facility. Mitchell liked San Francisco General. He liked June and Nualan, his nurses. He didn't want to move. This sent everyone—doctors, lawyers and burn specialists—into a flurry. But Mitchell didn't back down. He remained at San Francisco General.

With the hospital's chief of staff, Mitchell went over the constant barrage of painful pokes and prods. Not only did the chief of staff scale things back but he also promised Mitchell that every procedure would come with an explanation of how it was going to help Mitchell get out of the hospital. The poking and prodding didn't go away; neither did the pain. But by gaining a small amount of control, Mitchell was finally able to feel that he had some say in his life.

The plastic surgeon arrived at Mitchell's door one day.

"Mitchell," he said, "it's time we talked about your face. Your original face has been burned off. We need to make you a new one. What did you look like before? Do you have some pictures?"

The nurse gave the surgeon Mitchell's driver's license. He stared at the photo on the license for a while. He looked at Mitchell, and then he looked back at the license.

"Man," he said finally. "I know we can do better than this."

Mitchell laughed. He hadn't laughed in months.

Phoenix Rises

The man who survived the fire wasn't the same one who had been injured riding his motorcycle down Van Ness. He didn't look the same. He was short a few fingers. But he had a perspective on life he hadn't had before.

The new perspective was tested in those early days. After three months, Mitchell was walking around, getting into trouble. But because he still needed help with situations requiring hands, a staff member was always with him. He noticed that they subtly kept him away from any mirrors.

After the months since his accident, the folks around San Francisco General had grown used to his face. Armed with his new philosophy, Mitchell decided to see for himself what everyone else was seeing.

Using a clever ruse, Mitchell tricked June, his almost constant companion, out into the hallway. He was in front of the mirror before she realized what had happened.

The guy who looked back at him from the mirror that day looked nothing like what Mitchell looks like now. Livid scars crisscrossed his face. The patches of skin looked like they'd been clumsily assembled in the dark. His nose was partially collapsed; his eyes peered out of ragged holes.

"Woooo," he said to the mirror. "That's an interesting looking guy."

Well enough to leave the hospital, Mitchell moved in with Bea, who, like the nurses, was an everyday angel. Reality began to set in. With no fingers, and the remainder of Mitchell's hands so sensitive that even a stiff breeze induced agony, he couldn't feed himself, drive, turn on a TV, answer a phone, open a door or reach into a pocket. It was six months before he could use the bathroom without assistance.

Frustration ate at him. Even as a dashing gripman, Mitchell had experienced difficulty controlling his temper. Like the gasoline that changed his life, his anger lit quickly and burned hot. The weight of all the small things that he couldn't do almost broke him one day. He remembers collapsing, screaming and crying, staring at a doorknob he couldn't turn. The slippery, round surface taunted him. Then he kicked off his slippers, reached up with his feet and turned the knob.

The door opened, as did Mitchell's universe.

More than a shift in perspective, a simple turn of a doorknob revealed a universal imperative. *It isn't what happens to you, it's what you do with it.*

Dedicated to his new motto, one that he would eventually share with people all over the world, Mitchell met and overcame obstacles each day. He learned to eat with a fork strapped to his hand. Sure, the effort required different tools, but he was eating. It wasn't instantaneous success, but each challenge he overcame reinforced his new belief system.

Some challenges wouldn't be solved by mechanical ingenuity. Mitchell didn't spend much time out in public. He knew what people saw when they looked at him, and he saw the same thing in the mirror. The culture and media defined what was "normal" for both Mitchell and the strangers who saw him. He couldn't help but feel their judgment. In public, Mitchell did everything he could to avoid eye contact. He thought it was the kind thing to do. If he ignored them, maybe they would be spared the trauma of noticing him.

Sitting in front of the TV day after day, avoiding the judgment of strangers, was the easiest existence. After all, getting barbequed is tough on the system and sometimes the simple act of living left Mitchell exhausted. But Mitchell realized that he was closing the door to the universe by letting his face keep him prisoner. This would be his face for the rest of his life. It was time for the universe to get used to it.

"Monster"

Mitchell took his huge dog Puppy with him wherever he walked. Because the plastic surgeons kept emphasizing that he shouldn't get too much sun, he would always wear a wide-brimmed hat, usually his Smokey the Bear hat. A Great Dane walking next to an emaciated, burned up, fingerless guy with long hair and a drill instructor's hat on the boulevards of San Francisco wasn't a sight you'd see every day. In a city full of weird-looking people, especially in those heady Haight-Ashbury days, the sight of Mitchell and Puppy roaming the streets must have turned a few heads.

The agreement with his nurses when Mitchell left the hospital was that he'd come back to the hospital to work. He would make the rounds of burn patients, telling them things like, "Man, you're the only guy in this place who's as funny-looking as I am." Mitchell hoped it would bring some humor and perspective to the burn patients he met.

While Mitchell made his rounds, Puppy would sit, still as a statue, at the entrance of the hospital. His 125 pounds encouraged people to let him be. After one visit, he was making his way to where Puppy was sitting when a man who was staggering by, obviously inebriated, started berating Mitchell.

"God, you're a mess. Jesus, you're the ugliest thing I ever saw. What the hell do you think you're doing here? I'm gonna beat that ugly face of yours!"

Despite his intoxicated condition and the fact that he was probably twenty years older than Mitchell, there was no way

Mitchell could have won the fight. The old Mitchell—in superb physical shape, an excellent skier, a gripman, a guy who never had anything to fear—would have made short work of the drunk. But the new Mitchell wondered how he was going to deal with this man.

While Mitchell was silently considering his options, the drunk began escalating his actions. As the loudmouth prepared to get physical, Mitchell noticed that Puppy, drawn by his master's voice, had arrived on the scene.

"Look, I'm pretty messed up," Mitchell confessed. "I won't be much of a match for you. But would you like to fight my buddy?"

"Sure," said the inebriate.

"Puppy, come. I want you to meet this guy because he wants to fight with you."

The man took one look at the dog, froze for an instant and then took off.

Adapting meant thinking creatively. What would Mitchell have done if Puppy had not bounded up? Perhaps he would have started a conversation with the guy. Maybe he would have enlisted the aid of a bystander. He could have zipped back inside the hospital. Sometimes it takes living with a disability to see the numerous options that constantly surround us.

Mitchell's most disturbing encounter wasn't with a drunken bully. A more distressing situation confronted Mitchell as he walked Puppy past a school playground full of children.

A grade-schooler spotted him, shouted something to the

others and soon they all broke off their playing and ran to the fence to stare. Then, by twos and threes at first, but soon en masse, they began chanting.

"Monster, monster, monster, monster...."

Teachers immediately swooped down on their charges. They herded the kids away, scolding them as they went.

Mitchell felt lost. It wasn't that he was offended. It was a fact that he had to admit: He *did* resemble a monster. His looks were nothing if not dramatic. To a kid, he probably looked like Freddy Kruger with a few Frankenstein stitches thrown in.

The feeling of loss came from the hope for acceptance, despite his cinematic looks. More than anything, he wanted to show the world a vital truth: Someone who looks "monstrous" on the outside can be good, warm, funny and caring on the inside. In fact, they might even be someone you wind up liking as much as your best friend.

How could he communicate all these things to the kids on the playground? Chewing out those kids for their mass bullying would not be half as effective as personally showing them their honest mistake: A good person lived under all that scar tissue.

He'd survived the fire. With the help of his unofficial motto, he unlocked his mental prison. Maybe it was time to make his motto official. Maybe it was time to start sharing his message with people of all ages and abilities.

If Mitchell's motto was a seed, the reaction at the playground was the rain that caused it to germinate. But he needed to learn just a few more lessons before his message was ready to blossom.

You Can't Do That

It was time for the phoenix, once burned almost to death, to fly once more. Literally. He'd soloed on the very day of his accident, and flying again symbolized how far Mitchell had come in getting his life back.

As soon as Mitchell was able, he returned to ground school. To complete some goals, baby steps were necessary. He started his lessons early in his recovery, when he was still unable to feed himself. But the way he looked at it, feeding himself was about survival, not *living*. And whether or not he could feed himself had nothing to do with flying a plane. By the time he was flying with an instructor, he was still having issues with the buttons on his fly.

It's not that flying was easy. Planes were designed for ten digits. Even the cockpits of simple single-engine planes have at least thirty knobs and dials that need tending. That's not including the fuel controls, flap and rudder switches, and countless other instruments that require pokes and tweaks. For Mitchell, simply operating the radio meant using both hands to juggle the handset. This meant he had to take his hands off the control stick, a move not known to inspire confidence in one's passengers.

The instructor wanted to help, which is a natural response to someone with a disability. But Mitchell wanted to fly solo. With each session, he resolved to take over one more task previously completed by the instructor. After 50 hours of lesson time, Mitchell was flying as well as he had before the accident.

"When are you going to let me go solo?" he asked the instructor.

"I don't know if you will be allowed to solo," the instructor replied. "I'll have to check with the FAA."

On the phone with the FAA, the instructor tried explaining the situation. "This guy is a mess. You should see him."

"You mean he can't fly the plane?" the FAA responded.

"No, he flies the plane pretty well. But I don't think you should let him fly. You should see him. He's been burned all over his body! His fingers are gone!"

"Can he fly the plane?"

"Yes, yes. He flies the plane fine! But really, you wouldn't believe what he looks like!"

The conversation continued to circle much like a flying loop. Finally, the FAA's message sank in. We don't care what he looks like. We're not there. If he can fly the plane, let him fly the plane.

The next morning, Mitchell took his second solo flight. It felt even better than the first.

Not surprisingly, the lawyers began swarming around Mitchell's hospital room long before he regained consciousness.

This was not a case of a stiff neck from whiplash. The pain and suffering were abundantly clear. Eventually, the ambulance chasers were chased off. A friend recommended the legal services of Pat Coyle. By the time Mitchell was conscious enough to think about his injuries and what they meant for his future, the legal case was well underway.

Not only was Coyle a good lawyer, he became a friend to Mitchell. During Mitchell's hospital stay, Coyle occasionally stopped by his room. Sure, his case was a personal-injury lawyer's dream, but Mitchell felt a deeper connection. After all, there wasn't much for him to do, so they chatted, argued and got to know each other over time.

Confident in their case against both Honda and the company that owned the laundry truck, Coyle and his associates sued for a total of $2.75 million. That figure was based on the pity they were hoping to illicit using Mitchell's poor, ruined, hideous example of a body. After all, he would never be able to drive a car, hold a job or do anything but vegetate. The high sum would compensate Mitchell for a lifetime of lost earnings.

The problem was that it took two years to go to trial. By June 1973, there was little Mitchell couldn't do, and he didn't feel like throwing a pity party in the courtroom. The lawyers insisted he try appearing a little more affected by his injuries than usual. They assigned someone to attend to Mitchell at all times.

During one of the first hearings, Mitchell left to go to the men's room. He went in by himself, and when he came out, Coyle saw him and his face paled. He corralled Mitchell off to the side of a minor hallway and demanded, "What do you think you're doing?"

"I had to take a leak," Mitchell said.

"Did you realize that one of their lawyers was in there at the same time as you? From now on, I'll go in with you." After trying so hard for so long to become independent and to get on with his life, Mitchell felt that the trial experience was surreal at times.

The opposition focused on the fact that Mitchell was flying planes again and seemed to be fairly competent. Coyle responded by having a film made of Mitchell, highlighting all the things he couldn't do. According to our legal system, people who suffer an injury are awarded a larger amount the more helpless they are. The award is reduced depending upon how well they recover. In other words, people are rewarded monetarily for not recovering.

It's not that Mitchell felt conflicted about suing. His life had been seriously interrupted. Getting fried was not how he would have chosen to spend that afternoon. Scarred and fingerless was not how he would have chosen to spend the rest of his life. By the end of the proceedings, Mitchell realized that it was not his apparent helplessness but his friendliness and charm that were his greatest legal allies. The jury liked him; they may have even admired him. That, more than anything else, made the opposing attorneys eager to settle.

The truck driver's story conflicted with key eyewitness accounts and Mitchell's own account, which was that the two vehicles, both his motorcycle and the laundry truck, were heading north on Van Ness. As they crossed the intersection of 26th the laundry truck turned right onto 26th from the inside lane, causing Mitchell to drive into the side of the truck. The truck driver, however, claimed that Mitchell collided with the laundry truck as it traveled along 26th through the Van Ness intersection. One problem with the driver's story: the traffic on Van Ness had the green light. By claiming that he wasn't at fault because Mitchell hit him as the truck traveled on 26th through the intersection with Van Ness, the truck driver was admitting to running a red light. The driver created his own catch-22.

The case against Honda wasn't as simple. Mitchell's team theorized that in a front-end collision the gas cap can come undone with the movement of the rider across the gas tank (riders don't wear seat belts). Of course, Honda had expert witnesses testify to the safety of their tanks. They also provided a sample tank that their lawyer would occasionally smack with a mallet to enunciate a point: Their tanks were safe.

Mitchell's team hired an independent lab to do its own tests. In the lab, the team members didn't just crash the motorcycles; they added a simulated body to the tests. Honda, who had built a crash-proof tank, hadn't built a crash-proof gas cap.

Two weeks into the trial, the judge decided there should be a settlement conference. He feared an extreme outcome: Mitchell either wouldn't get any money or would get too much money, either of which would lead to endless appeals.

After this conference, Mitchell's lawyers gave him the news. Each of the defendants had offered $450,000. Mitchell's share of the $900,000, after legal fees, would be about $500,000. It was decision time. Should he shoot the dice and go for more? What if the decision favored his opponents and he wound up with nothing but legal bills? Mitchell had decided before the trial what he was going to do. This was "found" money. His life was okay. There was no point getting greedy.

He took the money.

Around the time of the trial, his lawyers could not believe that Mitchell was not seeing a shrink, so they made some appointments for him.

The group therapy counselor was a basket case. Mitchell quickly noticed that the man had enough of his own disorders to start a support group of one. The man was convinced of his own infallibility. Even worse, he'd managed to talk a few of the group members into this charade. Here were normal people who kept coming back to the same pushy know-it-all, some for four years. They were convinced that their own abilities of coping were inferior. From Mitchell's viewpoint, they were addicted to the idea that they were sick.

Mitchell believes that, indeed, psychology has its place in the world. Some people have scars that are so deep that they need more than a Swedish massage. But the type of therapy he experienced in his group sessions was worthless. In fact, it did more harm than good. As Mitchell puts it, "Sure, sometimes things don't feel good, you get pissed off, nobody likes you…Welcome aboard, nice to have you here on Spaceship Earth!"

Again, Mitchell found that people who wanted to help him were often trying to fit him into a box. Just because a traumatic accident had left him physically different didn't automatically mean he needed counseling.

Some people might spend years, even decades, focusing on the worst aspects of their lives. Their relationships never work out. Their jobs never go anywhere. They don't like how they look. Mitchell discovered that each person's life is about choices. Instead of thinking about all the bad things, why not focus on how good life can become? Do you want to talk only about how bad smoking is, or shall we focus on how wonderful fresh air and healthy lungs can be?

The idea of self-help groups should be just that—to help people understand that their decisions are up to them. As Mitchell sees it, you can also sleep on a bed of nails and wallop your forehead every half hour with a two-by-four if that's what you decide you "need." But wallowing in angst is not Mitchell's style, and that's what his group therapy sessions had been all about.

After a few sessions, Mitchell quit. He pointed out to the group that he didn't see the benefit of spending an hour a week thinking about problems he considered to be relatively minor when there was so much life that he should be out pursuing. Some of the folks gave him some pushback, but what really confused Mitchell was the counselor's response.

Sure, now, in 1973, Mitchell was doing well, the counselor explained. But if he didn't get long-term therapy, sooner or later he would jump out of a window.

Mitchell still hasn't jumped.

Where Everybody Knows Your Name

Mitchell loved being outdoors. He enjoyed the beaches in Hawaii, the streets of San Francisco and the slopes of Aspen, Colorado. He was back to flying, back to marching through the city with Puppy, and soon enough he wound up back on the sands of Hawaii. But he still wasn't able to participate in nature like he had. Anything gear-intensive, like skiing, wasn't a Mitchell-friendly activity. Instead of feeling the need to "do" something while he was in nature, Mitchell developed an appreciation for nature by simply watching.

Mitchell's love of nature is matched with an equal love of people, but the constant introductions to new people and repeatedly telling the same story were starting to get to him. He wanted to send out a universal memo with the subject line, "What happened to me and why I want everyone to get over it." The initial novelty of being able to walk around San Francisco was wearing off. Strangers weren't to blame. He understood their curiosity. But he didn't want to get resentful, either. If he could just find a place where, once everyone knew him and knew his story, people could start learning about the person underneath the burns.

Mitchell's love of natural beauty and his search for a small community led him to Crested Butte, Colorado. An old coal-mining town nestled in the Rockies at almost 9,000 feet, Crested Butte is 25 miles in a straight line from Aspen. If one wanted to drive from Aspen to Crested Butte, it would add 217 miles to a car's odometer. It was just about as remote as one could get while staying in the first forty-eight states. Surrounding the valley of Crested Butte are soaring, snowy peaks, including Crested Butte Mountain. Because no miner had found precious metals in the 12,000 foot stand-alone peak, she sat unspoiled, to be enjoyed by anyone looking for the perfect blend of nature and seclusion.

In Crested Butte, Mitchell found freedom and the treasure of the scenery. The year-round population hovered around 600 souls. Using his settlement money, Mitchell became a citizen of the town.

Once townspeople heard Mitchell's story, they would soon forget about his physical appearance. Well, that's what Mitchell hoped would happen. He didn't really slow down long enough to check. After he bought one of the nicest of the old Victorian homes left from the town's mining days, he bought a share of the largest commercial building in town. A local bar went under, and Mitchell decided that it was the perfect time to get into the saloon business. He added a few more properties to his real estate portfolio and, suddenly, life in Crested Butte was booming. Tired of Aspen's steep prices, snow bunnies started looking around Colorado for more affordable vacation spots.

Several small towns, Crested Butte among them, perfectly fit the bill. Some vacationers fell in love with the sleepy community and stuck around. Mitchell's investments were paying off.

The best investment Mitchell made, however, was also his wildest. A friend managed to talk him into investing in a way of manufacturing a new type of fuel-burning stove. At first, the endeavor sounded a little too high-risk for Mitchell. Someone always knew someone who was about to invent the next best bread-slicer. But as his friend raved about these new, almost fifty-percent efficient, wood-burning stoves, Mitchell started thinking. The country was in the middle of an energy crisis. Cars were lining up at gas stations. By the time the first production model of the new stove was available, Mitchell had invested almost sixty-five thousand dollars and was named the chairman of the board. The title did more than look good on his resume. As the lone businessman in a company of inventors, he kept busy. The little company could barely keep models in stores.

Mitchell's investment returned millions to his bank account. His financial advisor stopped complaining about all the money he had invested in this harebrained invention. The generous return on his investment meant virtually limitless possibilities. This phoenix could soar.

Mitchell bought his very own plane, a Cessna 206, the station wagon of the skies. Flying is an expensive hobby, even for millionaires, so every time he needed to fly somewhere, Mitchell ran a classified ad to see if anyone needed a lift. For fuel money and some companionship, folks around Crested

Butte could fly wherever Mitchell was headed that day.

On Veteran's Day in 1975, Mitchell and four locals prepared the Cessna at nearby Gunnison Airport. It was just fifteen degrees on the ground and, with no heated hangers, the plane required some deicing. If there was one thing Mitchell had learned while getting his commercial, multi-engine and instrument certifications, it was that pilots never fly with ice on the wings.

After using several deicing techniques, Mitchell loaded the Cessna and taxied to the end of the runway. It lifted into the air. The plane was climbing fine. Twenty-five feet. Fifty feet. At 75 feet, something was wrong. The plane was not climbing as quickly as it should.

Mitchell found out later that the wings of his aircraft were covered with a thin sheet of ice, which weighed the plane down and impeded its climbing ability. He was running out of runway. Mitchell decided to put the Cessna back down. When he reduced the throttle, the plane lost its forward momentum and stalled, plummeting towards the runway.

Mitchell screamed, "Hang on!"

The Cessna didn't nose over, it just fell flat, as if the fingers keeping it in the air had simply let go. When it pancaked into the ground, the landing-gear support broke on one side of the plane. The uneven tilt caused gasoline from the topped-off tanks to spill out the overflow vents. Fuel spilled down the wings. No way, thought Mitchell, not again. He quickly killed the engine and flipped all the electrical switches to "off."

"Get out!" Mitchell yelled at his passengers. "Everyone out now!" They didn't need any more instruction.

As scared as he was of fire, Mitchell seemed stuck. He couldn't move his legs. His back hurt. A lot. No fire started, but Mitchell's fear of another inferno was subsiding as he grew more concerned about his legs.

The medics came, heard about his symptoms and carefully extracted him from the Cessna. Once he was in the hospital, the doctors tried every test imaginable. On the third day, the neurosurgeon came to deliver the news. He would not walk again. Miracles could happen, but the doctor's prognosis was that he was going to need a wheelchair for the rest of his life.

Mitchell still can't remember how he responded. He remembers trying to keep up the facade of the burn victim who doesn't let anyone or anything get in his way, but inside he was devastated.

What did it mean? No one else from the plane crash was hurt as badly as he had been. During one test they had even opened up his spinal cord to see how badly the cord was damaged. It looked fine. The doctors determined it was a simple bruise to the nerves in the spine that had taken his legs from him.

Mitchell lay in his hospital bed, once again wondering what possible future he could have. As they had before, friends and well-wishers came to see him. Phone calls, letters, and cookies arrived from Crested Butte. One day, nearly four weeks after the accident, a young woman called him.

"Mitchell, I hear you're not doing very well. I wonder if

you remember when I had some problems, you told me something I'll never forget. You said, 'It's not what happens to you, it's what you do about it.' Do you still believe that, Mitchell?" she asked.

It was almost as bad as looking in the mirror that first time. Didn't people get that he just wanted to be left alone, to bathe in his own misery? Yes, they were his words, but the latest episode in Mitchell's life was beyond bearable. Life had been great as a handsome, modern-day swashbuckler. When a fire tried to turn him into a Hollywood monster, after some mental calisthenics he'd turned that disaster into an asset. Now he loses his legs?

Mitchell reflected upon what he had said. His self-taught coping mechanisms started coming back. Why would losing the use of his legs succeed in destroying him when the inferno failed?

He decided that he would never rule out the possibility of complete recovery. The human body is a fragile yet amazing machine. Bruises on the skin heal. With the right technology, other tissues can heal. But he wasn't going to wait for the cure to come to him. He was going to live life, in or out of a wheelchair. He started by taking control.

Recovery meant more hospital time and more therapy. But this stay was going to be different. Mitchell organized happy hours. After a long fight with the staff, he had a private phone put into his room. If he wasn't ready to be out in the world yet, then the world would come to him.

Another wheelchair-bound patient at the hospital worried Mitchell. He was nineteen and had only partial use of his arms. Until he became paralyzed, he'd lived a life that sounded familiar to Mitchell. He participated in almost every outdoor activity under the sun. Yet Mitchell watched him sit in therapy like an emotionless stone statue, completing his exercises like meaningless chores. Mitchell understood how the young man was thinking. No one signs up for life in a wheelchair. He decided to say something.

During a therapy session, Mitchell rolled up to the young man. "Before all of this happened to me," he said, "there were ten thousand things I could do. Now there are nine thousand. I could dwell on the one thousand that I can't do. But I prefer to think about the nine thousand that are left."

It's a choice everyone, including Mitchell, must make every day.

In true Mitchell style, when he thought he was well enough to take on the world again, Mitchell checked himself out of the hospital.

Firewalk

The period of Mitchell's life after his second near-fatal accident was both busy yet more sedate. He still lived by his own rules, deciding for himself where and what he could do in his wheelchair. As the trajectory of his life stopped taking near-fatal plunges, he got suckered into politics. The mayor of Crested

Butte sat down at Mitchell's bar and, in the Tom Sawyer way of any good small-town politician, coerced Mitchell into taking over a vacant city council seat.

Then AMAX came to town.

At the time the largest mining company in the world, AMAX had been making noises about mining nearby Mount Emmons, which the locals called the Red Lady because sunset turned its slopes a brilliant red. AMAX was looking for molybdenum, an elusive ore used in everything from aircraft engines to bicycles. Because mines are usually located near poor, rural communities that would welcome an economic boost despite what might be done to the nearby environment, the multinational firm figured Crested Butte to be another pushover.

AMAX didn't figure on the will of the Crested Butte community. They didn't figure that Mitchell, dedicated to the preservation of the mountain wilderness and the town's drinking water, would run for mayor to prevent an environmental tragedy.

He not only ran for mayor, he won.

Not a stranger to adversity, Mitchell and the town began an all-out war. They filed legal briefs citing old Colorado laws giving a town the right to control its watershed. They tried new legal strategies, some of which became precedents for future environmental law. Mitchell brought the media into the fight, and he didn't pull any punches. *Time* wrote a story titled, "Battle over the Red Lady: A Colorado Shangri-La in a Classic Struggle against Development."

Mitchell became Crested Butte's biggest lobbyist. He

had meetings in the halls of Congress and in the West Wing of the White House. In the end, Crested Butte won. The bottom fell out of the molybdenum market and AMAX moved on to another village. Crested Butte thanked Mitchell by voting for his opponent in the 1982 mayoral election. When they needed Mitchell for city council, he didn't think he wanted the job. When he wanted to stay on as mayor, the town told him he was ready for bigger things.

Thinking that his true calling was politics, Mitchell's next fight was for Colorado's Third District Congressional seat. Again, he struggled in an uphill battle against political insiders and the public's prejudice. He made speeches, gave interviews and tried to shake every hand in the Third District twice.

"He's not just another pretty face," almost became Mitchell's campaign slogan. It lost to "There's nothing he can't do," which was not nearly as funny. However, it was what Mitchell believed, especially after winning the primary as a political nobody.

Although he didn't win the general election, he still felt like a victor. He learned that running for Congress is worth at least three Ph.D.s. He also came away with a glowing endorsement from *Rolling Stone* magazine:

> This guy is a little weird and wonderfully original,
> and I hope he gets elected to Congress. That assembly
> seems permanently overpopulated by fools and
> knaves, hacks and drones, the TV hot-dogs who hide

behind blow-dry hairdos and vacant smiles. The Capitol would be staggered by the mere presence of this man's indomitable spirit.

After all the work that went into fighting AMAX and running for Congress, Mitchell finally got around to taking care of himself. He went in for an operation to fix a problem he was having with his eyelids. Still recovering, a friend of Mitchell's called from Arizona. The friend had been attending a Tony Robbins seminar. He explained that he'd told Robbins about Mitchell's life, and both his friend and Robbins wanted Mitchell in Arizona. Right now. Mitchell explained how it was impossible, that his eyes were sewn shut, but they wouldn't take no for an answer.

With only one eyelid partially open, Mitchell arrived in Arizona. Robbins didn't want to simply meet him; he wanted Mitchell to speak at the seminar. Again, Robbins and his staff wouldn't take no for an answer. After his speech, in which he told his life story and what philosophy he'd used to get his life back on track, they invited him to stay.

Three days after he arrived, firewalking night rolled around. Three beds of mesquite coals ranging from twelve to forty feet long were prepared. Mitchell stood about eight feet away; the heat was so intense, he was worried it would somehow affect the plastic surgery that had just been done on him. Members of Robbins' staff backed up his wheelchair as a precaution.

He only wanted to watch. Not being able to walk made

the idea of the firewalk a little hard to digest. Not only that, but he'd had enough experience with fire to last a lifetime.

The concept is that if you can walk on fire, you will prove to yourself that you can do nearly anything, because any limitations in your life are self-imposed. This was a lesson Mitchell had learned—twice.

People started walking over the coals. As they emerged, they were exultant. No one was burned.

Mitchell suddenly found himself at the end of a bed of coals, taking off his shoes and socks and saying to Tony and a friend, "One of you grab me under the right arm, one under the left. Lift me up and turn me around, because we are going to do this backwards." And they did.

Mitchell had more contact with the coals than anyone else. While the other workshop participants had stepped over the coals, his feet were literally dragged through them. When he got to the other side, Mitchell could see the two dark trails where his heels had gone. He didn't feel the coals, but he was numb from the waist down anyway. More significantly, he did not have a single burn.

A lot of scientists are skeptical that anything mystical is involved in this exercise. Elaborate theories about perspiration on the feet repelling the heat, similar to touching a wet finger to a hot iron without being burned, have been proposed to explain the phenomenon. These theories might be true, although Mitchell's feet had significant contact with the coals.

Magical, mystical or scientific, the experience is a potent

metaphor. It is a visible illustration of the power of the mind and how that power can be used to break down a perceived barrier.

Phoenix Speaks

The speech at the Robbins seminar was Mitchell's first inspirational talk. He had always been good at speaking off the cuff. The hundreds of political speeches, the talks he had given on disability issues, his testimonies before Congress and other committees, and countless interviews all came together. Without a formal speech, he started out by simply telling groups his story: the funny parts, the tough parts, the triumphant parts.

People loved it.

Everyone has scars. It's a part of life. Not all scars are as visible as Mitchell's, but physical and emotional trauma can cripple anyone. So Mitchell talked about refusing to let scars keep us prisoners.

More and more, he was being asked to speak to various groups. Mitchell spoke before environmental groups, handicap advocacy groups and several Congressional committees considering environmental legislation. The direction of his life was crystallized when a woman approached him in a supermarket. She'd heard of Mitchell's story and was wondering if he would speak at a convention for temporary employment agencies. Mitchell wavered. Employment agencies? Then she mentioned it paid two hundred dollars. A two-hundred-dollar check and a free meal to boot! He took the gig.

By the fall of 1987, he realized that he had a wonderful

159

opportunity. He saw that he could make his living by doing something that he had previously done for free. Though their patronage lets him earn a living, corporate seminars are not his favorite speaking jobs. Neither are the large gatherings in hotel ballrooms. His favorite place to speak is the barn at the Griffith Center near Denver, where he speaks for free.

The Griffith Center is a place for kids who society has thrown on the junk pile. These youngsters have been beaten, abused, neglected, and discarded. The center is their last chance. Their experience in life has taught them, directly and indirectly, that life is stacked against them. They expect the worst from people and know that helping others invites pain and exploitation.

And then they see Mitchell: mutilated face, no fingers, in a wheelchair. Yet they see a happy man, a man who has every excuse in the world to be miserable and somehow refuses to use any of them.

Every time Mitchell speaks at the Griffith Center, he thinks about that day years ago when he walked by the playground and heard the chant of "Monster! Monster!" He remembers the sadness, the longing to quiet those kids' voices, to speak to them gently and tell them his story.

Mitchell's wish came true. He's talking to them, and they're not yelling at him. Now they're paying close attention to Mitchell's words. He tells them about his accidents. He explains, in great detail, the many opportunities he's had to quit, and how and why he refused to take them.

Mitchell gives the kids other examples of everyday heroes. He tells them about John Thompson, an eighteen-year-old North Dakota farm boy who was on the farm by himself doing his chores one day. Thompson started the auger, a huge screw inside a cylinder that carries grain into a silo. His untucked shirttail got caught in the auger, which began pulling him into the machinery.

Although he fought the equipment, Thompson found himself on the ground, no longer in the auger's grip. He saw that his right arm was gone. He noticed most of his left arm was gone. Not good. He ran up the hill to his house. With what little was left of one of his arms, he struggled to open the sliding glass door. No luck. He ran around to the corner of the house and finally managed to get the screen door open.

In the kitchen, Thompson knocked the phone off the cradle and tried punching the buttons with his nose. It didn't work. He found a pencil, picked it up in his teeth, and pressed buttons on the phone with the eraser. He called his cousin. When the cousin answered, Thompson shouted, "This is John! Get help, quickly!" With a remarkably clear head, he picked up the receiver with his teeth and hung up. They shared a party line. If he didn't break the connection, his cousin couldn't make a call.

Then, John Thompson, an average kid who got average grades, went into the bathroom and sat in the bathtub so that he wouldn't bleed on his mother's rug.

When the medics arrived, the sight of the bleeding, armless torso shook the medics so badly that Thompson had to calm them down. He explained where his arms were, that there was ice in the refrigerator and where to find garbage bags. Amazingly, doctors reattached his arms in a six-hour operation. When, weeks later, a reporter asked him how it felt to be a hero, the question baffled him.

"I did what anyone would have done."

Mitchell makes the same point in his speeches. He's a regular guy. He has the same resources everyone else has. There's no special training that turns people into heroes. Heroes only have superpowers in comic books. A heroic life is really a matter of choice. That's Mitchell's message: anyone can be a hero.

The magic occurs when his audiences of young people, with their strong bodies and active minds, understand the significance of Mitchell's life and he knows that he's gotten through to them in time.

When he first spoke at the Griffith Center, Mitchell didn't know much about the place. As he drove there, he became self-conscious and worried that a speech for adults might not translate to a younger audience. When he finished his talk, he could plainly see that he had made an impact as he surveyed the faces looking back at him. But the final confirmation—the biggest payday of his career—was the reaction of a thirteen-year-old kid from the inner city who, with tears in his eyes, came up to Mitchell after the speech.

The young man told Mitchell that he had tried to commit suicide three times. Mitchell was amazed at his story. Then, the boy said, if he ever felt like doing something like that again, he would remember what Mitchell had said that day.

As Mitchell listened, tears welled in his eyes, too.

The memory of walking by that playground and hearing the chant of "Monster!" occasionally comes back to Mitchell. By the time those children in the school yard saw him, he had already achieved many small and large victories. He'd recovered his self-respect, which was why the chant didn't offend him. Mitchell realized that they weren't chanting their judgment of him as a person but merely about how he looked. Still, he remembers feeling an overwhelming desire to show them the truth: Someone who looks monstrous on the outside can be good, warm, funny and caring on the inside.

And the "monster" could become your best friend.

That's why Mitchell speaks.

Source Material*

Mitchell, W. "And That's Why I Speak." www.wmitchell.com.

———. "Breaking the Barriers." www.wmitchell.com.

———. "Choice Is Yours, The." www.wmitchell.com.

———. "*It's Not What Happens To You, It's What You Do About It.*" Arvada,CO: Phoenix Press, 1999.

———. "My Biggest Fee Ever." www.wmitchell.com.

———. "Never Ever, Say Never." www.wmitchell.com.

———. "Take Responsibility for Your Life." www.wmitchell.com.

———. "Why I Travel the World Speaking to People." www.wmitchell.com.

*Used with permission from W Mitchell

His Eyes and Her Hands
The Davey and Vera Hulse Story

Davey

It was Labor Day, 1960. Davey Hulse was seven and about to start second grade. His brother Danny was ten and was getting ready for the fourth grade. They lived in Dufur, Oregon, just down the road from where I would one day grow up. Their dad, Bill Hulse, was a wheat farmer and, like many dads are to their sons, the two boys' hero. A story Davey already knew by heart at age seven was how his dad, at six years old, fell off a swinging gate and broke both his arms and his jaw. When it came time to take the casts off, the doctor accidentally slid the wrong side of the scissors under one of the casts. Bill didn't flinch—he didn't say a thing. It wasn't until the doctor cracked the cast open and saw all the blood that anyone realized something was wrong. After telling the story Bill would rub his jaw and say, with a slow smile, that before that accident he had a much more symmetrical face.

Danny and Davey wanted to grow up to be just like their dad. Danny was in his first motor vehicle accident at age five when he rolled the tractor. By Labor Day of 1960 he had been licensed to hunt with a shotgun for a year.

When their dad mentioned that he needed to go out to his recently leased farm to look at the moisture depth in preparation for seeding fall wheat, Danny's ears perked up. The

Frailey place had several outbuildings that were perfect hideouts for birds, mice and squirrels. They would be ripe for exploring by the ten-year-old master hunter and his seven-year-old spotter.

With school starting the next day, their mom wasn't too keen on the idea. But Danny made his protests known. It wasn't the day before school, Danny argued, it was the last day of summer. Davey made the same argument and soon the two were jumping into their dad's truck, pellet gun in Danny's hands.

While their dad practiced the science of farming, the two Hulse boys explored several old sheds and checked around the granaries for signs of rodent activity. Danny noticed an old shop that had a huge, heavy, sliding wood door. The possibilities of finding rodents behind that door looked better than the disused sheds and boring old grain storage. The two boys pulled, pushed and strained to get the door open. When it was open just enough to let the boys in they found a treasure trove of nuts, bolts, pieces of pipe, and even better—mice nests.

Among these fascinating discoveries, Danny found real treasure: a small tin with a lid like a paint can. The label on the can was yellowed, deteriorated paper and the two boys could only make out the word *Gold*. They picked it up and gave it a shake. It rattled. A can with *Gold* on the label that rattles!

A nail and a piece of pipe–an impromptu hammer and lever–were found close by. Danny set the can on the oak work bench and started tapping the nail under the rim of the lid. Ever mindful of their father's advice, Davey stood behind Danny and to the left as he hammered. He peered over his older brother's shoulder, anxious to see what treasure it contained.

Danny and Davey didn't realize that in the old can they were holding were old Gold Label blasting caps, probably made with lead azide. Unlike so many commodities, when lead azide blasting caps age they don't lose their potency or go "bad." In fact, if lead azide sits around long enough and, especially if it is exposed to moisture, it can turn into copper azide salt, which is an extremely unstable chemical.

The last thing Davey remembered was a loud explosion.

Bill Hulse was in an unplowed wheat field about a mile away when he heard an explosion. As he sprinted towards the workshop from his pickup truck, Davey came to and started calling out to his brother. He was confused and couldn't see anything. Then he heard his dad's soft voice.

"Boys."

The next thing Davey remembered was feeling the clean grass under his fingers and the warm sun on his face. They were outside. A truck sped off and soon his dad was back with a neighbor who was a trained nurse. Hearing how badly the boys were injured, she had called the hospital in The Dalles, about an hour away and set up a rendezvous with an ambulance in Dufur. She also phoned a neighbor to ask that she call the kids' Mom and get her headed toward the hospital in The Dalles.

As they rode towards Dufur in the back of his dad's pickup, Davey remembers his brother talking about how cold he was. When the ambulance to which they had transferred in Dufur arrived in The Dalles, their mom was waiting. For the next three days she spent most of her time in Danny's hospital room. His injuries were catastrophic, but when Danny was conscious he would ask his mom about Davey. Out of kindness she lied, telling him that his brother was fine. Danny had experienced enough pain without her adding to his worries.

Three days after the accident, Danny died from his wounds.

Just as life changes in an instant, it goes on. When he was finally able to check on his own farm, Bill Hulse found that neighbors and friends from all over had taken care of the everyday chores. These were people he had helped over the years with their own mundane chores and earth-shattering catastrophes.

The superficial damage to Davey's face healed but his ability to quickly grow scar tissue became a problem. The shrapnel from the can of blasting caps had blinded one of his eyes and while he still had partial vision in the second eye, a piece of shrapnel was embedded next to his retina. The piece of metal and the scar tissue buildup around it were eroding away the little vision he had. Surgery at a hospital in St. Louis was unsuccessful.

Davey Hulse was seven years old. He'd just lost his brother and he was blind.

At this point in little Davey's recovery, his parents could have reacted in several different ways. In their grief over the loss of their first son they could have ignored the needs of Davey, focusing instead on what they had lost. With a newly-blinded child, they could have become super safety-conscious. Families have been torn apart by less catastrophic accidents, but this was not the Hulse family's way. Through a mixture of support, pragmatism and love, they survived the tragedy and moved on with their lives. To this day, Davey talks about his parents' sacrificial love, which was constant and unwavering.

The most important question for Davey's parents to answer was what he was going to do with his life now that he couldn't see. Farming was out. Sure, there were things he could do around a working farm or ranch, but there were better ways to make a living. Rural life was hard enough with undamaged vision.

In January the Hulses went to Portland to visit the Oregon Commission for the Blind and learn what kinds of jobs blind people could do. Using blind labor, the Commission operated two production lines, a cane furniture shop and an ammunition factory. Davey thought the idea of working at a bullet factory sounded interesting. Life as a blind factory worker was not what his dad had in mind for Davey. Bill Hulse didn't like what he'd seen. On the drive home he swore that Davey would never work in "a place like that."

So it was off to Oregon's School for the Blind in Salem.

At the OSB, a boarding school for anyone who didn't live in Salem, the seven-year-old was adjusting to more than just the loss of sight. This was the first time he had been away from his parents for an extended period of time. While Davey was there, about one hundred students attended the school. The majority of the kids were blind because of the pure oxygen used in premature baby incubators. Pure oxygen caused an overgrowth of the retina that could result in blindness. The second-leading cause of his classmates' blindness was a measles epidemic. Davey, with his blindness caused by a traumatic accident, was in the minority. Approximately eight million Americans have visual impairments; about three million of those are legally blind, and about 200,000 read braille.

After a weekend with his family either in Dufur or on the coast where they would travel in a seventeen-foot trailer, Davey would think about the long drive back to Salem and internally cringe. But, as hard as it was for himself, the emotions his parents must have felt were beyond Davey's imagination.

Adjusting to blindness and the boarding school life wasn't seamless. Davey came from a lifestyle where he had been encouraged to take risks and stand up for himself. Conflicts with other students didn't always translate to peaceful deferment. Blind or otherwise, if you pushed Davey's buttons, he stood up for himself and sometimes he let his fists do the talking. He didn't think blindness was something others should hide behind.

Jason (not his real name) was a fellow student particularly good at pushing Davey's buttons. One minute they'd be best friends, the next they'd be grappling on the floor. In what was thought to be a clever solution to the fighting, the administration decided the two boys should bunk together. After a particularly heated "disagreement," Jason was left unconscious. That's when the administration came up with a more clever solution: they decided to keep the two separated. Just like the feisty yet easily-forgiving younger version of himself, Davey remains long-distance friends with Jason.

By sixth grade Davey was wrestling for OSB. He was sixty-two pounds and four feet tall, wrestling in a weight class where boys could have thirty pounds on him. But that didn't matter to Davey. Wrestling was a perfect sport for him. His opponent had to be in constant physical contact and he often felt the other boy's movements before there was any visual cue. By the end of his sixth grade year, Davey had made it to three wrestling tournaments.

Davey left Oregon School for the Blind in 1966 after the sixth grade. He had made some friends for life at OSB. He knew how to read braille, type braille and type on a regular keyboard. But when Davey left Salem, he also left with certain intangibles. As hard as his time there was, he says, even now, that he wouldn't change the experience for the world. He left as an older version of the same scrappy seven-year-old, yet tempered and disciplined.

He jumped back into life in Dufur. His mom took him horseback riding and read him the notes while he played his trumpet. While he'd been in Salem, Bill had received his pilot's license in hopes that, by flying to and from Salem, he could reduce travel time. Because of the typically poor weather in the Willamette Valley, that didn't work out as well as Bill had hoped. But, now that Davey was living in Dufur, flying became a way to bond. On Sunday mornings Davey and Bill would wake up early and survey the ranch by air.

Through the various music groups Davey joined as a trumpet player, he took two group trips to Europe. It was risky. As difficult as it was for them to trust that he would be safe in his endeavors, Davey's parents encouraged him to take risks. It was the only way he'd learn independence.

Stints of independence as a teenager were promising but didn't answer the bigger question of what Davey was going to do for work. After high school he went to Northwest Christian University. While he was studying for his Bachelor's degree, he took a job as a youth pastor. Davey realized that, while the ministry was not for him, the opportunity to counsel people through difficult experiences was rewarding. He enjoyed helping people find ways to succeed in their lives. Maybe this was a piece of the puzzle to Davey's future.

When he transferred to Western Oregon University just down the road in Monmouth, Oregon, Davey decided he would study social sciences with an emphasis on corrections. Then, while interning at the Employment Department, Davey met Mark Barrall, a vocational rehabilitation counselor. Mark explained that employment counselors could help people figure out what careers would suit their talents; on the other hand, vocational counselors not only helped people figure out which direction to go but also the counselor had a modest budget to assist with their classes or equipment if needed.

Davey was inspired. This was a way to provide concrete help to people who needed it and were actively looking for ways to improve their lives. Davey decided that, like Mark, he would get his Master's in Vocational Rehabilitation from the University of Northern Colorado.

After three years at NWCU where he married his first wife, he transferred to Western Oregon University where he completed his Bachelor's Degree. Davey returned to Oregon in 1978 from Colorado with a newly inked Master's degree. The State of Oregon hired him as a Vocational Rehabilitation Counselor for the Bend Vocational Rehabilitation office.

Davey was finally back in Eastern Oregon. He was doing a job that he loved, helping people that, in many ways, were like himself. It was during his time in Bend that he met Juan, a man who had recently broken his back and couldn't work at his old job any more. Juan was an educated man with contacts throughout the community. His prospects for finding a new line of work looked good to Davey.

Life for Juan, however, had become one disappointment after another. It wasn't just his inability to find a job. Before his injury, Juan loved to fish. But now he had to use a wheelchair and the only wheelchair-accessible places to fish were usually packed with amateur anglers and over-fished. When Davey usually saw Juan he was in a world-beaten mood.

Yet one day Juan showed up to an appointment with Davey in a world-beating mood. Davey had to ask: what changed?

Just up river from Prineville, Juan had gone fishing and caught a lunker! Davey knew that section of the river, though, and there weren't any bridges or docks that would allow wheelchair access.

Juan had his friend hold on to his wheelchair as he went down the embankment, acting as brakes and a counterweight. They fished for a while and, when Juan had finally caught his lunker, the friends attached the truck winch to the back of his wheelchair and the biggest of the group hand-cranked Juan up the embankment backwards.

It was a small success, but it overshadowed the other disappointments in Juan's life. Soon he had a job as a bookkeeper for a friend's business.

Davey was having his own successes. He had a loving wife who, just prior to his taking the job in Bend, gave birth to a baby girl. Over the course of 17 years with the State, he applied for ever more responsible jobs, winding up as the ADA Coordinator for Senior and Disabled Services Division. Life was good and steadily getting better.

Vera

Vera Randall grew up on a Minnesota farm in the 1950s as the oldest of three children. It was the stereotypically 1950s farm lifestyle, and, though Vera was a good and obedient girl, she always knew that her life would take its own path. At three she pretended to play the piano, knowing that some day she wouldn't be pretending. Sure enough, she grew into an accomplished pianist, playing organ in church and eventually playing piano for soloists, musical groups and special occasions while she attended Moorhead State University.

When Vera first arrived at Moorhead, she intended to study accounting. Then she got her first quarter schedule. The classes mandated by her degree started first thing in the morning. There had to be something else, she thought, something she was interested in but that didn't require waking up at obscene hours of the morning. She settled on English with a minor in Speech & Drama.

Like many college-educated young women of her generation, Vera went to work as a secretary and typist. What might have been a career in the corporate world ended one November evening in Montana. Vera was 26 and about to be married when she, her fiancé and some other friends took a trip to Montana to hunt elk in the Bitterroot forest. One night, while they were trying to warm their tent with a stove, the tent caught fire. Vera survived the fire but suffered burns over roughly seventy percent of her body.

At first, thanks to shock, the extent of her injuries wasn't obvious. Her fiancé, who'd managed to escape from the tent with superficial injuries, realized quickly that Vera was badly burned. After contacting emergency personnel on his CB radio, they met an ambulance halfway and Vera was taken to a hospital in Hamilton, Montana.

Realizing the severity of her burns, the hospital in Hamilton arranged an airlift to Harborview Hospital in Seattle, Washington. Heavily sedated, Vera doesn't remember much from her time in the burn unit though she still remembers hearing the screams from down the hall. At the time, Vera decided that she was hearing students rehearsing for a play. She'd been told that Harborview was a teaching hospital. The way she figured it, hospitals are often attached to universities and, as a former drama student, she knew that repetitive screaming could be easily explained as rehearsal. It made more sense than the alternative.

With their exposure to the flames, Vera's hands bore most of the fire's wrath. After her burns healed, she began rehabilitation to learn to use the few fingers she had left. She would eventually have surgery back in St. Paul to provide better dexterity to her hands and fingers.

The suicide rate for people with the severity of burns Vera had is very high. Suicide wasn't for Vera. Her life wasn't going to center around her medical condition. Vera had a future to look forward to.

Finally healthy, Vera realized she was out of a job. She couldn't type fast enough to be a secretary. Not only could she not type as fast, she had lost some of her ability to play the piano, a skill she'd had for as long as she'd remembered. Beyond the mental and physical trauma, the loss of both personal and professional abilities could have led to a downward spiral of disappointments and depression.

Vera put the accident behind her and moved on. She decided it was time to find another profession.

A news director from a local television station saw something of a news hound in Vera. He hired her to produce investigative stories for the evening news. His instincts proved accurate. She loved going undercover. It reminded her of improvising scenes in drama class. Vera's passion and drive eventually led to several investigative reporting awards.

Vera recalls one story in particular about a school for mentally-challenged people who were basically warehoused. One girl aged 16, kept in restraints, became pregnant. Vera received other reports of very suspicious criminal behavior. Her report resulted in a full-blown law enforcement investigation in 1978.

Vera could have gone on with her investigative reporting career. Who knew where she might have wound up. With her quiet determination and sharp mind, she would probably have landed in a major market like New York. But two things obstructed that career path. While she was working as a segment producer, she visited some friends in Oregon and fell in love with the state. She also realized that representing both sides of a news story was getting frustrating. When a person or company was doing something wrong, she wanted to be able to do something besides simply giving the public a "fair and balanced" news story.

So Vera went back to school to get her degree in law. She was thirty-five when she graduated and, looking around Minnesota, felt that there might be better opportunities to represent the underdog somewhere else. With no attachments, no fiancé and a new law degree in hand, Vera felt like she was starting a new life. What better place to begin anew than in

Oregon's Willamette Valley.

Her Hands and His Eyes

For Davey Hulse, 1985 wasn't going well. That was the year his marriage ended. It was also the year he was laid off from the Oregon Vocational Rehabilitation Division. As much as he'd wanted to make the marriage work, especially for his daughter Darah, the divorce meant that he could put the misery and frustration of the marriage behind him. The divorce also meant that he could move to where there was work. The State of Oregon soon re-hired Davey as a vocational rehabilitation counselor in Salem.

Davey made sure that Darah was a priority. When he wasn't working, he was traveling to Bend to see her. He also had some free time to sign up for state-sponsored seminars. In September 1985, Davey signed up for a training seminar hosted at a hotel on the coast.

At that time, Vera Randall was working for Disability Determination Services under the Oregon Vocational Rehabilitation Division. In fact, she'd helped put together the seminar that Davey was attending that September. She remembers looking down from where she was sitting on the "experts" panel and seeing in the crowd a ruggedly attractive guy with a white cane. Before the seminar was over and she could return to the conference room floor, the man she had seen was gone. She wouldn't see him for the rest of the seminar.

The very next weekend as Vera was waiting in the

Greyhound bus station in Salem to catch a bus over to visit friends in Bend, she saw the same man. She wasn't going to let him slip away this time, so she introduced herself, explaining that she had seen him at the recent seminar. He told her that he was waiting for the bus to Bend so he could spend the weekend with his daughter, but that it was running behind schedule. When the bus finally arrived, they chatted all the way to their destination. By the time they'd reached Bend, they'd made tentative plans to have lunch in the future.

Vera waited for two weeks for Davey to call. Nothing. Her patience exhausted, she looked up his information in the state's directory and called him at his office.

"You said you were going to call me and we were going to get lunch," Vera said, getting right to the point. "So do you want to get a pizza or what?"

Davey Hulse, not a fool, said yes. Maybe 1985 wouldn't be that bad of a year after all.

In August of 1986, almost a year they met, Vera and Davey married.

Davey remembers a tough and demanding job working as a ward manager at the Oregon State Hospital, Oregon's public mental hospital. On a day in 1988 when he was home listening to daytime television, an advertisement caught his attention. The pitch was for a weekend seminar that would provide all the information needed to start making money from real estate. Davey knew from his upbringing that there was no such thing as money for free, but he also knew that you didn't make money without taking a risk. When he retired from his state job, he'd have a pension, but that would be in twenty years. His current year-and-a-half job already felt like a lifetime. When Vera came home, he asked her if she'd be interested in attending the seminar just to see what "no money down" really meant. She was interested.

Davey and Vera liked what they heard at the seminar. "Nothing" actually meant three percent down, but after looking at several properties in Salem they found a parcel with two houses and decided to invest.

On weekends Vera and Davey maintained and improved the rentals. Vera was the eyes, Davey the hands. Unlike the work that the two did during the week, their weekend projects produced concrete results that were both rewarding and profitable. Their rental company grew through development and reinvestment. By 1992 the only necessary activity for Vera was picking up the rent checks from the post office each month. One month, as Vera completed that task, she remembered the rewarding work they used to do. *This is boring*, she thought to herself. It was time to find their next project.

When Vera prompted Davey about what kind of business he would be interested in starting, Davey thought about the question of supply and demand. At the time, in 1992, Davey was working as the Americans with Disabilities Act (ADA) coordinator for the Senior and Disabled Services Division of the Oregon Department of Human Services. Because of his work at DHS, Davey knew how hard it was to find alternatives to print formats—large type, audio and braille. There was a definite demand for alternate format publications and it was likely to increase due to the Americans with Disabilities Act that had recently gone into effect.

With a borrowed braille embosser, the two converted a small basement room into the headquarters of their new company: Braille Plus, Inc. Eighteen years later, their little project has grown into a company of ten full-time employees working in five-thousand square feet of offices and production space. Davey and Vera, once again working as a team, created another successful company that went far beyond its humble beginnings.

The Touch of Yarn

If the success of their two businesses wasn't enough, an odd requirement from Vera prompted another project. As they talked about retiring—or at least not working on day-to-day operations—Vera told Davey that he needed a hobby. Davey is the kind of guy who doesn't like sitting still, and Vera knew that he wouldn't stay retired for long if he didn't have something to do. Davey agreed with her and decided to take up knitting. It was something he could do with his hands while they enjoyed a more leisurely lifestyle. The only problem was that Davey couldn't find a simple, sight-free way to teach himself how to knit.

Instead of giving up, as many beginning knitters have done, Davey used a variety of resources, including an online community of blind knitters, to teach himself. Then he wrote a book, the book he wished he could have had at the beginning. Lion Brand Yarn, one of the most well-known brands of yarn used by knitters, offered to publish Davey's book, *The Touch of Yarn*, so that both blind and sighted beginners could find a simple, logical resource to learn knitting.

Not All Work and No Play

Life for this dynamic duo is not all about keeping their noses to the grindstone and inspiring others by their work ethic or good deeds. A few years ago, they began to take ballroom dance classes through private teachers and the local community college. The couple learned how to use their complementary assets and years of working together in other physical activities to acquire the skills needed to waltz or cha-cha around town and around the world. They firmly believe in the saying, "Dance like no one's watching …."

It's a tossup whether it's dancing or traveling that ranks higher as their joint hobby. When they can dance as they travel, they're happiest. Their scrapbooks include photos and souvenirs from all over the world, including China, South Korea, Hawaii, Alaska, the United Kingdom, Scandinavia and many countries in Europe. A favorite snapshot shows the couple dancing on a river cruise through Paris on the Seine. On their French vacation, they floated past Notre Dame Cathedral. Rising from their dinner table, they danced in the aisle to a waltz.

These days Davey divides his working time between knitting projects, Braille Plus and developing better solutions for sight-disabled people. Vera juggles her duties as landlord and President of Braille Plus, Inc. while toying with new ideas for another business. Davey and Vera, people who have faced difficult physical challenges, built their successes first as individuals and then as a team. They've been together for decades and this team doesn't sound like they're ready to retire.

Major Success is Built on Small Victories

As a blind, vocational rehabilitation counselor, Davey has both experience and insight into how to turn physical disability into success.

The foundation of success is support. For Davey, support started with his family but gradually included his friends at school, then rehabilitation professionals and finally his wife. It's important to remember that support isn't exclusively family and friends; it can come from any direction.

Often the first step on the road to success is taking control. In Davey's case, his parents took control and yet, at the same time, they gave up control. The first thing they decided was that their injured son wasn't going to come home and live a protected, safe life. He was going to go out and take risks, learn some hard lessons and live. Because of his parents' choices early on, when it came time to take control of his own life, Davey was well-prepared.

"Getting out of the morass" is what Davey calls the biggest problem in people's lives. The morass is something everyone struggles with from time to time, and Davey has observed people struggle with it all his life. What he's learned is that success is built on success. At first, one needs to define success as a series of small steps. Don't get distracted by the big picture, by what can and can't be done. Think about what can be achieved in the moment and in the day.

Success is defined by each person. Juan, Davey's client in Bend, liked fishing. But Juan was stuck in the morass, unable to move his life forward after an injury. After he rediscovered the small joy of catching a fish, Juan was starting a new career and moved out of the morass.

When we're in the process of recovering and rebuilding, the first success might be microscopic. But it's important to find one small thing that can be achieved. Succeed at that one thing, and go to the next small thing. This breaks the cycle of attempting to succeed at big things, failing, then experiencing the emotional fallout of that failure. Creating that small success breaks the cycle, which takes us away from the morass. Success builds on success until self-esteem is raised to such a level that what couldn't be done becomes almost a memory.

Davey's one last piece of advice: Don't be stoic. Don't be afraid to ask for help. Knitting an afghan for his mom was a big success built on several small successes, but if Davey hadn't asked for help, he never would have made it to the last stitch.

With her eyes and his hands, the Hulses prove that disabilities need not be impediments to living full, loving and happy lives.

Source Material

Hulse, Davey. "Davey Remembers." Letter written to Jake French.

Lynn, Capi. "Instructions Didn't Help, So He Wrote His Own Book."
Statesman Journal. March 7, 2010.

State of Oregon. "Blasting Caps." Oregon State Police: Arson and Explosives
Section. http://www.oregon.gov/OSP/AES/Blasting_Caps.shtml

Shot Happens
The Mike Schlappi Story

Mike Schlappi and I have a lot in common. We were both injured when we were young and we were both injured by friends. We've also both spent time thinking about how paralysis has affected our lives, and we've come to the same conclusion: Success and happiness are defined on our own terms.

Like my own story and the stories of many in this book, Mike has lived a life of ups and downs. Mike is always moving. He's a medal-winning paralympian, father and successful speaker. When he has a chance to sit down to think, Mike seems to be constantly evaluating his emotions, his attitude and how those relate to circumstances.

Shot Happens

Mike's journey down the path of athlete-philosopher began on Veteran's Day in 1977 just before he turned 15. He had already demonstrated his athletic gifts on his high school football and basketball teams. On that Veteran's Day, he was running over to his friend Torrey's house to hang out. When he arrived, he found Torrey still getting ready, so Mike walked through their house while he waited. Torrey's dad was a police officer, and his off-duty revolver was on the nightstand. Succumbing to his natural teenage curiosity, Mike picked the gun up. As he did, Torrey came into the bedroom to announce that he was ready to go. Before either boy had time to consider the rules for safe gun handling and what could go wrong, Torrey had taken the gun out of Mike's hands, hastily emptied the cylinder of live ammunition, pointed it at Mike's chest and pulled the trigger, never expecting the gun to actually fire.

The unexpected happened.

Hit in the chest at point blank range with a .38 special slug, Mike should have died instantly. But he didn't. The bullet missed his heart by a miraculous margin. The slug itself even missed his spine. Unfortunately the bullet's travel through Mike's body generated a shock wave that was especially damaging to soft tissue. By passing so close to his spine, the shock wave from the bullet damaged his spinal cord, causing instant paralysis. From that moment forward Mike would never be able to move or feel anything below his waist.

Mike doesn't recall much of the first few weeks of recovery though his disposition must have impressed his caretakers. Before he left the hospital, he received a "Patient of the Month" award for his positive attitude. Still, his parents were cautioned that his attitude was a bubble destined to pop. Therapists warned Mike's family that it was normal for newly paralyzed patients to go through a grief cycle of denial and despair before full mental recovery. They were told to expect feelings of intense frustration that could lead to screaming fits. While Mike remembers feeling the occasional stomach-sinking sensation of despair, he found ways to keep his mind distracted. It wasn't about simply keeping his physical body active; it was about keeping his mind occupied. He took responsibility for his mental state with daily self-prescribed doses of what he called "attitude therapy." This meant that he would give himself a day to memorize a poem or phrase. Sometimes, if he felt his thoughts spiraling out of control, he would close his eyes and focus on what he had instead of what he had lost.

Burgers & Chores

Mike's mental exercises didn't stop when he left the hospital. When he arrived home he had expected to take advantage of the sympathy he knew he would be getting from his family. That didn't happen. His parents, determined to keep his life as unchanged as possible, worked out a plan to keep him growing towards independence. This plan wasn't explained to Mike, but soon he got the picture. They made sure he had his fair share of tasks awaiting him when he rolled through the door. His parents called it attitude therapy. Mike called them chores. But by treating Mike as a normal, contributing member of the family—just as he had been before the shooting—Mike had no other choice than to act like a normal, contributing member of the family.

The Schlappis had a big house and some property to maintain, including a garden and orchard. Mike had always been a willing helper, and Mike's family still needed his help. Though he didn't necessarily complete the chores in the same way or in the same amount of time as he had before, he still did the dishes, cleaned the bathroom, fixed sprinkler heads and sorted fruit, among other things. It wasn't fun, and the first few attempts at doing a chore in a wheelchair-friendly way could get downright frustrating. But each success built on itself until Mike realized he was just as able in a wheelchair as he'd been before the shooting.

The one area Mike's mom cut him some slack was piano lessons. Mike told his mom he could no longer play piano because he couldn't work the pedals. In an amazing exercise of discretion, Mike's mom decided to concede this particular battle and told him he no longer had to take lessons. Mike says that almost made it worth getting shot.

Another activity he discovered to add to his attitude therapy was wheelchair sports. Even if Mike started feeling sorry for himself, between the sports and the chores he didn't have much time to indulge in self-pity. Mike's coaches reinforced the lessons he was learning at home. It was fine to have a bad day; not everyone has a perfect game or perfect day. However, using a bad experience to justify having a bad life was something neither Mike's coaches nor his parents were going to let pass.

Even in the early stages of his recovery, Mike began to realize that his emotional reactions often depended on how he perceived a certain situation. He still did normal teenage stuff, and most of his friends treated him no differently after the shooting. They went cruising, throwing him into the back seat and tossing his wheelchair into the trunk. Once when they drove to the local burger joint, they all got out of the car to order their burgers and fries. Mike watched from the backseat as they ate fries by the dozens and flirted with girls. They'd forgotten him.

Mike didn't mind because he didn't see their forgetfulness as rudeness or insensitivity. They thought of him as uninjured—normal—and the slight inconvenience caused by his friends was worth the realization that they didn't think of him as being different.

Learning these lessons early in his life and so quickly after his injury made Mike think about the meaning and implications of a bad attitude versus a good attitude, both in his mind and in practice.

Naked Water Skiing and Self-Pity

Mike remembers the sensation of the lake water as he jumped in. It was a couple of years after the shooting accident. The only part of his body that actually felt cold was from his stomach up, leaving the lower part of his trunk and legs feeling comparatively warm like he was wearing half a wetsuit. Clad in a life vest and lime green swim trunks, Mike was bobbing behind his family's boat, which would eventually be towing him through the water on an improvised boogie-board.

At Mike's sign the boat started accelerating. Soon he found himself barely able to hang on to the piece of plywood as the boat dragged him through the water. This wasn't water skiing. Mike was beginning to doubt that he was having much fun. Buffeted by wave after wave of water, he started to lose his bearings. He could make out the people in the boat ahead of him watching and laughing. He had a good sense of humor, but he didn't know what they were laughing at. Folks on the shore were staring and pointing. He didn't feel like laughing, and this wasn't what he'd signed up for. He looked behind, checking how badly his legs were flopping around. That's when he realized that the water had torn his shorts off.

Mike let go of the plywood board and let his legs sink until he was simply floating, waiting for his dad to turn the boat around to pick him up. He wasn't having fun anymore. Not only was he not having fun, he was embarrassed, more embarrassed then he'd ever been in his wheelchair.

Mike felt like blaming somebody. He wanted to blame the bullet. He wanted to blame the gun. He wanted to blame his friend Torrey. But he couldn't. He could only blame himself, because he realized as he bobbed in the water waiting for the boat to return that this was the perfect example of what his life would be like. Situations would arise where he would feel embarrassed, in pain or powerless. Who would he blame then? Would blaming the bullet, the gun or his friend improve the situation?

He couldn't change the effect of the shooting, he could only change how he would respond to it.

It was an epiphany for Mike, an epiphany he would work on refining for the rest of his life. It would inspire speeches and a book. More importantly, it would change his approach to life.

Medals

In 2000 Mike joined the USA Paralympic Basketball team once more on the world stage. Over the past 16 years Mike had won two gold and one bronze medal. He was competing for his fourth time for his fourth medal. Team USA made it all the way to the semifinals, where they played against a talented and successful team from Holland. Recovering from a 14-point deficit at halftime, Team USA's final game-winning 3-point shot didn't make it through the basket. Once more they would be playing their final game for the bronze.

The last seconds of Mike's final Paralympic game couldn't have been more dramatic if it had been written in Hollywood. The score was tied. Great Britain had the ball and missed a lay-up. Getting their rebound, one of the young USA players sped his wheelchair down the court and launched the ball at the hoop from 35 feet away. The ball swished through the net just as the final buzzer sounded. The 20,000 fans went crazy. Mike found himself at the bottom of a human and titanium dog pile.

Afterward, thinking about the victory, Mike felt a sense of incomparable achievement. Yet, his medal track record was gold, gold, bronze and now bronze again. After receiving his first bronze medal just four years earlier, Mike remembered feeling defeated as if winning the bronze meant losing the gold. This time was different. Mike felt like he had *won* the bronze. The shift in perspective changed his entire outlook on the Paralympic experience that year. He came home feeling like a hero instead of an also-ran. His simple shift in perspective caused a shift in attitude which, in turn, caused a change in his mood.

Attitude and Mood

Mike has used a shift in perception and a positive attitude to change both the real and perceived outcome in many life experiences. What he has personally discovered and exemplified in his life is that a difference between attitude and mood exists. Wearing a smile 24 hours a day doesn't improve your chances of success or happiness if feelings of depression, doubt or guilt are hiding behind that smile.

Mike has found that having a positive attitude is what makes a real difference. For those of us who don't always have a good day or don't always have a smile to wear, this is good news. He explains that you don't always have to be in a good mood to have a good attitude. In fact, suppressing feelings in order to fake a good mood can cause a worsening in attitude. Everyone can have a bad minute, hour or day. It's having a positive attitude that helps us see past those feelings to see the larger picture.

When Mike takes in the big picture, he sees his athletic achievements - his tennis championships and basketball medals. He sees his wife, Tami, and their five kids. He sees the awards and accolades he's won as a public speaker. And, like me, he looks at a future spent sitting in a wheelchair. Yet when he takes in the big picture with a positive attitude, he's thankful for all the good things that he has in his life.

*Source Material**

Schlappi, Mike. *Shot Happens*. Brigham Distributing. 2009.

*Used with permission from Mike Schlappi

This Is What It's Like to Die
The Wally Szempruch Story

Walter Szempruch isn't a household name. He didn't invent a slicing-dicing kitchen gadget. He doesn't have a grill named after him. However, if you've been to the hospital in the last two decades or watched a medical show on TV, you've seen his inventions. His quietly brilliant career at Abbott Laboratories wasn't about infomercials or fame. He represents the countless inventors industriously working every day to make people's lives safer and healthier. A modest man, Szempruch downplays the importance of his inventions.

Not only have the products he worked on—like flexible plastic IV bags—been of use to medical professionals but also they have helped save lives by decreasing the likelihood of contamination during medical procedures. If it had not been for the care Szempruch himself received in the hospital early in life, this talented inventor wouldn't have been around to contribute to the life-saving efforts of our medical community.

Wally was born in 1949 in Chicago to Chester and MaryAnn Szempruch. He joined his three older siblings, Lawrence, Patricia and Diane in their modest northwest Chicago home. Chester, a World War II veteran, had immigrated from Poland in the mid-1930s to find a better life in the U.S. After he left the service, Wally's dad found work as a tradesman and carpenter. Wally's parents understood the value of education and though finding the money in their budget was a struggle, they saved enough to send their children to the local parochial school, St. Hyacinth's Basilica.

Growing up in the 1950s, Wally soon became fascinated by America's fledgling space program. Several nuns at St. Hyacinth's encouraged the amateur scientist. In junior high, one of the big scholastic events of the year was the science fair. Combining his love for science and skill in engineering, Wally built a Redstone rocket replica about nine feet tall for his seventh-grade science project. Made from corrugated cardboard, white paper and scale-accurate decals, the rocket took a month to build and earned him a ribbon. Continuing the NASA theme, Wally assembled a four-foot replica of the Gemini capsule for his eighth grade science project. Again, the model took him about a month to build, but its tin plating and painted-wood escape tower looked like a scaled-down version of the real thing.

When it came time to choose his high school, Wally's eighth grade teacher encouraged him to apply to Lane Technical High School. Lane Tech was a magnet public school with vocational classes and a reputation for high academic standards. It sounded like a perfect match for Wally's developing interests.

In the 1950s and '60s, scientists were the new national heroes. Scientists had developed the atomic bomb, atomic power and transistor radios, and they'd discovered what DNA, the blueprint for life, actually looked like. Astronauts would someday step off the shoulders of scientists onto the moon. It seemed that there was nothing these slide-ruler-wielding heroes couldn't do. They were even beating once incurable diseases. It was no wonder that kids across America like Wally were thinking of pursuing science as a career.

When he was still in grade school, Wally heard grownups talking about polio, a disease that still hadn't been slain by the biologist warriors. Kids seemed to be by far the most susceptible. Even scarier, the heroic scientists didn't seem to have many answers. Why did reported cases spike during the summer? Why did some people develop antibodies to the virus without showing any symptoms? Why did the flu-like symptoms develop into paralysis in some children and not others? After 1952, when tens of thousands of polio cases were reported and thousands died, the race for an effective polio inoculation became a national imperative.

Jonas Salk is credited with developing the first effective polio inoculation in 1955. Administered by injection, the Salk vaccine used dead virus cells as a way of prompting the body to create antibodies that recognized the virus. Kids across America, Wally Szempruch included, were given Salk inoculations. Another polio specialist named Albert Sabin announced a different approach. His vaccine used live samples of the virus that had been crippled to the point of harmlessness to prompt the same immune response. The theory was that the weakened virus was too weak to cause illness yet healthy enough to still be contagious. Scientists hoped that this would cause a secondary immunization in people who hadn't yet been inoculated.

Factors besides the effectiveness of the two vaccines

caused a switch in public health policy. In what is still considered a controversial decision, health officials selected the attenuated Sabin vaccine over the Salk vaccine as the best weapon against polio. Inoculations containing the dead virus were phased out and soon kids were lining up for an oral dose of coated sugar cubes of the weakened virus.

By the fall of 1964, Wally was a sophomore at Lane Technical and a member of the Junior Reserve Officers' Training Corps (JROTC) program. He remembers lining up with his fellow cadets in the auditorium one day in October to take the cube. Already inoculated, polio was the furthest thing from Wally's mind. It was just one more of those governmental "Department of Redundancy Department" procedures that seemed wasteful yet harmless. His mind kept alternating between his promotion to Temporary 2nd Lieutenant Cadet and an upcoming school dance. That day Wally took his laced sugar cube along with every other Lane Tech student and promptly forgot about it.

When Wally made plans to go to the dance with a girl he'd met from nearby Alvernia Catholic, all thoughts of promotions, science projects and school work were soon forgotten. But before the date of the dance arrived, Wally came down with a nasty flu. He tried weathering it, hoping that the symptoms would pass in time for his date. Soon he was so weak he could hardly make it to school. By late November of 1964, Wally could hardly walk.

All the cute girls in Chicago weren't going to get Wally

to the dance.

Mrs. Szempruch had enough. It was the middle of December and Wally still wasn't better. She asked Dr. Sokowski, who had looked after Wally's older sisters, to make a house call. After a cursory exam, the doctor cradled Wally in his arms and folded his body, bringing Wally's head to his knees. It was everything Wally could do to keep from screaming. His back was on fire. Knowing that the pain was caused by a polio-inflamed spinal cord and back muscles, Dr. Sokowski told the Szempruchs that Wally needed to be admitted to the only hospital with an iron lung in Chicago: Cook County Contagious Hospital.

Wally, his brother Larry and Larry's friend Chuck drove to the hospital in Larry's blue Oldsmobile. Wally was cold. He had already lost thirty pounds. At the gate to the hospital, the guard didn't seem like he was going to let them in. Chuck made some choice comments, then picked Wally out of the back seat and carried him into the emergency room.

Once in his hospital bed, Wally found that though he could hold down food his body was getting weaker. He lay there on one of his first nights and noticed the lights through his eyelids dimming. His breathing grew shallow and more difficult. He exhaled and felt peaceful.

I might be dying, Wally realized. *So this is what it's like to die,* he thought. *This isn't so bad.*

That's when a nurse pulled up his eyelids, checked his pupils and began resuscitating him. To this day, he doesn't know the name of the nurse who saved his life.

A flurry of activity around the room woke Wally up to the point that he could see several people surrounding his bed. He realized that he was in an iron lung. The iron lung was gray, long and narrow. It made a continuous rhythmic sound as it pulled air in and then vacuumed it out. Wally couldn't help but think that if the noise stopped his life would be over. He likened his predicament to that of an airplane passenger praying that the sound of the engines wouldn't stop at 30,000 feet. At the tender age of 15, he found himself wondering if the iron lung could be redesigned to make it less intimidating and quieter.

Wally has thought about that peaceful moment since then. Why didn't he die? Was there a purpose yet unfulfilled? A young man went into the iron lung, and a future biomedical scientist would come out.

When Wally had enough strength in his body to be taken out of the iron lung, he was down to 90 pounds. By then the hospital staff had done enough tests to determine that he had succumbed to an infection of coxsackievirus, which is a type of polio. The muscles in his limbs had atrophied to the point where he was essentially paralyzed.

The family heard about an experimental rehabilitation program at Chicago's Wesley Hospital. After initially denying him entrance to the program, the hospital's administration was finally persuaded by a Szempruch family friend to admit Wally. While he was there, Wally made friends with a rehab patient and practicing psychiatrist named Dr. Bader, who was undergoing therapy for a congenital and eventually terminal disability. When they were getting to know one another, Wally asked him about his progress and chances of recovery. Dr. Bader replied honestly that he had no illusions about his chances. He was a doctor and knew what the future held. Respecting his new friend's honesty, Wally asked Dr. Bader for his evaluation of his chances. In his same no-nonsense style, Dr. Bader told Wally that besides doing absolutely fine with both his mental and physical recovery, Wally's optimism and outlook made him a joy to be around. All things considered, he added, Wally was handling his situation quite well.

Dr. Bader's words reinforced the physical rewards Wally was seeing in therapy. His mobility didn't come back overnight. It took months of excruciating exercises to restore the lost muscle. Though the use of his limbs was restored, Wally's legs were never as strong as they had been. Yet even the ability to walk with a limp felt like unconditional victory to the teen. The act of persevering against long odds became a cornerstone in Wally's life. From then on, he felt he could do anything if he put his mind to it.

By the end of his inpatient therapy, Wally felt a great indebtedness to his friends and to the staff who helped him get better. He felt he had to do something with his life to pay them back for how well they had taken care of him. Settling into a mediocre life would feel like failure. He lived his life as if they were still watching, and he felt that he had to make them proud.

The Chicago public schools sent a teacher to help Wally restart his education when he was still recovering. After rehab, he was able to attend school but, having fallen far behind his class, he enrolled in summer school.

Limping into summer school, Wally knew that people would stare, would know that he was different. When kids stared or a room quieted as he limped in, Wally tried to remember that they weren't gawking because they thought he was weird or a freak. They were thinking, "There, but for the grace of God, go I." Keeping this in mind helped him put his physical disabilities in perspective: It's okay to be different.

Eventually Wally outgrew his concern about what people thought of him. He realized that if he succumbed to self-consciousness he would miss out on so much of what life has to offer. Instead, Wally embraced life. He learned how to drive a car at 16. He learned to ride motorcycles. He learned to adapt, be resourceful and to persevere.

The two classes he took the summer after rehab helped Wally make up for the time lost in the hospital. His body still wasn't fully recovered—after two blocks of walking, Wally felt like passing out—but high school graduation wouldn't wait. By studying hard and taking extra classes, he managed to catch up enough with his classmates to graduate on time in 1967.

Wally was accepted into the University of Illinois at Chicago Circle (now University of Illinois at Chicago) and hoped to do well enough to get into medical school after graduating. Unfortunately, even with his extra class load in high school, once classes started Wally realized that his math skills weren't at the level they needed to be. He dropped out.

With his academic plans on hold, Wally was able to find a job at Baxter Travenol Laboratories. It was there that he found a professional niche that used both his scientific and mechanical skills. He enrolled in Wright Junior College and took math classes after his work day ended at Baxter Travenol.

In 1971, in the midst of working at Baxter and taking classes, Wally married Kathie Hanich. With a new wife, advanced math skills and some money saved from his work at Baxter, Wally was re-accepted to the University of Illinois and graduated in 1974 with a major in biology and minor in chemistry. At the end of 1974, Wally was scooped up by Baxter's competitor, the Hospital Products Division of Abbott Laboratories, now known as Hospira.

Wally arrived at Abbott Laboratories with purpose. He'd scratched his initial plans to attend medical school. Instead, he found what he was looking for in the challenges of a lab. He wasn't providing patient care from the bedside, but he felt like finding technical solutions to medical problems was indirectly helping both medical staff and patients alike. While he was still in college and working at Baxter Travenol, Wally invented a nasal cannula, the attachment that supplies oxygen from a tube to the nose. Wally had been bitten by the inventor bug.

At Abbott Wally was able to use the talents he'd developed in chemistry, biology and engineering to contribute and eventually lead research and development opportunities to the benefit of patients in need all over the world. Over the twenty-seven years he worked for Abbott, Wally and his R & D co-workers found solutions to everyday problems in the health care industry. They discovered an improvement to dialysis equipment that helped reduce the likelihood of infection in patients. Wally also invented a tamper evident seal— more as a precaution against accidental opening than intentional contamination—to indicate when an intravenous drug solution has been opened.

Another project Wally took on was finding a better way to feed patients intravenously when their digestive systems aren't working. The method for getting large volumes of the important "stuff" (amino acids, lipids, dextrose) into patients' bodies was already standardized. But Wally found that adding small doses of nutrients to the high-volume mixture was problematic. During his initial research, Wally stood in a hospital pharmacy and watched as staff added, by needle and syringe, small portions of nutrients to each large bag. He watched as sterile packaging piled up in the garbage. Back at the laboratory, his co-workers developed an electro-mechanical pump that worked similarly to a soft-drink dispenser which restaurant patrons sometimes see in bartenders' hands. When finished, Wally and his co-workers had a product that allowed staff to accurately deliver the desired micro-nutrients to the IV feeding bag.

Throughout the 1990s, Wally worked on a better design for intravenous solution bags (which are often seen suspended upside down next to patients' hospital beds). Instead of the IV products on the market that allowed permeation of oxygen and moisture into the bag, decreasing sterility and shelf life, Wally and his Abbott co-workers designed an improved attachment port that kept the sterile barrier intact.

After executives at Abbott decided to pursue market-ready acquisitions and, as a result, close down much of their in-house research and development efforts, Wally decided to take advantage of an early retirement package. By then he had almost a dozen patents to his name and had received several professional awards. Wally still works at Abbott as an independent contractor, helping their diagnostic division with documentation.

Wally has spent much of his life helping others, people he'll never meet, get better, safer health care. As his patent list shows, Wally has helped win a few more battles since his almost tragic struggle with polio. Still, there have been setbacks, both personal and professional. While he was still working in research and development at Abbott, he failed to get the funding needed to pursue a mechanical treatment method for cancer. One can only wonder what hope it might have provided the cancer victims who need it most. This professional setback was especially hard to take since the very personal loss of his first wife to breast cancer in 1999. Yet, like so many who have narrowly survived death, Wally takes a truly long-range view of his success in life. What makes him most proud aren't the professional contributions to medical science but the way he and Kathie raised their two sons, Kristofer and Kurt.

Wally and Kathie reared Kris and Kurt, born in 1979 and 1983 respectively, to value self-reliance and education. While the boys were growing up, Wally enjoyed the roll of being a bleacher dad. He has every one of their football games and wrestling matches on tape. By supporting their interests in sports, he felt that they would realize the value of team work, perseverance and competition that would sustain them in later life. Wally also taught them the principles that he had learned to value, such as the importance of being responsible for one's own physical, mental and spiritual health. As Wally learned, the world throws a lot at you. A healthy body, mind and soul are the keys to overcoming life's challenges.

Above all, Wally always taught them that honesty was the best way to maintain their integrity with others. The luxury of going to sleep at night with an unblemished conscience is not worth a single stolen item, broken contract or immoral act.

Though his lost battles are never far from his mind, Wally isn't upset by them. Nor does he do much boasting about his contributions to the medical community. Given the growing toehold of infectious diseases like MRSA and other penicillin-resistant bacteria, the improvements that Wally has made to both equipment and procedures may have helped countless patients avoid a serious or life-threatening disease.

But don't call Wally a hero. He doesn't see himself as such. All he admits to is doing a little more than most, yet not as much as others. He sees himself as a hard worker with some talent in science and engineering, a polio survivor who has tried to give a little back to the medical professionals who helped save a skinny Polish kid from the Northwest side of Chicago.

Source Material

Oshinki, David M., *Polio: An American Story*. Oxford University Press US. 2005.

Szempruch, Walter. Interviews via phone and email.

New Beginnings

Life is unpredictable. What I know for sure is that each of us will experience great happiness as well as great challenges. What I also have learned is that what happens to you isn't as important as how you respond to what life throws your way. No matter our circumstances, each of us is given the chance to begin anew each day.

It's difficult to summarize all of the lessons that the everyday heroes profiled in this book can teach us, yet the common themes are worth repeating here. Whatever your challenges, whether they are large or small, I hope that you'll recall how valuable these ideas have been for others who face huge challenges every day. I believe that incorporating them into your daily life can make your journey easier and worthwhile.

Believe that your life has purpose. Life is all about choices and your life is what you make of it. Each of us must struggle to achieve our full potential. Just as living a life that matters is a choice, choosing to be happy is an important part of creating a successful, fulfilling life.

Maintain a positive, can-do attitude. Of course, each of us will have bad days when negativity rules and our emotions take a roller-coaster ride. But remember that the mind is a powerful asset and you can master your attitude. In fact, you are the only person who can control how you view the world.

Focus on what you can do, not what you can't do. You decide what your limitations are. Appreciate the gifts that you have, and then ask yourself how you can put them to use.

The time to live is now. Think of each morning as a new beginning, a fresh start, a time when you decide how you will make a difference in your life and the lives of others. Stay in the moment and experience life with all of its ups and downs. Face what life hands you one day at a time and don't lose sight of what's important to you. Prioritize your goals and sincerely pursue them each day.

Never give up. You have strength inside yourself that's undiscovered and untapped. Remain hopeful and become more determined each day to reach the goals you set for yourself. And don't forget that we are all in this life together. Some goals can be reached alone while some require the help of others.

Honor people as they are and for what's inside of them. Accept the uniqueness of every individual and open your heart to the good qualities each of us has.

No matter what our plans are, life happens. It's up to each of us to live the life we've been given to its fullest. I wish you much happiness and success in your journey.

Contact Information

If you would like to invite Jake French to speak to your organization, association or at a special event, please contact us.

Email: jake@JakeFrenchInspires.com

Website: www.JakeFrenchInspires.com

Address: LIFE HAPPENS—Live It!
                79405 Shellrock Road
                Dufur, Oregon 97021

Phone: (541) 993-3359

To order additional books online, go to Amazon.com.

For quantity discounts on 15 or more books, email your request to:

jake@JakeFrenchInspires.com.

Thank you.